GRIN&
SHARE IT

GRIN&
SHARE IT

Raising a Family with a Sense of Humor

■ ■ ■

Janene Wolsey Baadsgaard

Deseret Book Company
Salt Lake City, Utah

Library of Congress Cataloging-in-Publication Data
  Baadsgaard, Janene Wolsey.
      Grin and share it : raising a family with a sense of humor /
  Janene Wolsey Baadsgaard.
          p.   cm.
      ISBN 1-57345-472-9
      1. Child rearing–United States–Anecdotes.   2. Motherhood–
  United States–Anecdotes.   3. Family–United States–Anecdotes.
  I. Title.
  HO769.B15   1999
  649'.1–dc21   98-51030
                                                                       CIP

Printed in the United States of America
10 9   8   7   6   5   4   3   2   1   18961 – 6438

For all those who taught me to dance!

Contents

Chapter One

If You Keep Both Feet on the Ground, You Can't Get Your Pants On

One Sunday when I was a newlywed, I noticed a large family

file into the chapel and fill the pew in front of me. The

mother's dress was half-unzipped, and several of the

children looked like they'd been thrown into the dryer without a static control sheet. The baby, perched on the father's hip, was drooling on his shoulder. Childless and naive, I took one look at that frazzled family and decided that when I became a parent, I'd have things a little more under control. I tapped the befuddled mother on the shoulder as I zipped up her dress. "Been one of those mornings, huh?" I asked.

"My mother told me I'd have days like this," she answered, shaking her head. "But she never told me they'd last for years."

An elderly woman behind me leaned forward. "Just remember, ladies," she said, grinning, "if you keep both feet on the ground, you can't get your pants on."

"Oh . . ." I answered, smiling politely. I didn't get it. Of course, I didn't get it. I was never going to show up for church with my dress unzipped. I never had any trouble getting my pants on.

Now—twenty years and nine children later—I get it.

Keeping both feet on the ground generally refers to seriously facing responsibilities with good judgment, determination, and hard work. In real life, that serious feeling often translates into devoting ourselves to bringing up the ideal *image* of a Mormon family. Sometimes this serious approach fails to take into account the fact that individual family members have a divine right to agency and seldom conform to the ideal. Raising a family is more like jumping on a roller coaster where we're laughing one minute and scared to death the next. The real trick is to find out what frees us up to enjoy the ride.

Often we feel like my four-year-old son Joseph the day I caught him punching his younger brother Jacob. "Joseph," I said firmly, "in this family we don't hit each other when we have problems or when we get mad; we talk about it."

Feeling awful about what he'd just done, Joseph lowered his eyes and grumbled back to me, "Why did I have to come down from heaven, anyway?"

"Well, Joseph," I answered, "when you were in heaven, you shouted for joy because you were so happy about your chance to come down to earth and get a body and experience everything here."

"Oh yeah?" Joseph answered. "Well, if I did, I was just teasing."

Joseph expresses well what most of us feel when we're faced with family life on the uphill side, like that first big hill on the roller-coaster ride. We find ourselves wondering, "Why did I want to come on this ride? I must have been crazy."

"Men are, that they might have joy," the Book of Mormon tells us (2 Nephi 2:25). I'm pretty sure that verse refers to all of us, men and women and children alike. Do we believe it? Do we really believe that the reason we exist here is to experience joy? Then why are most of us so serious all the time?

Maybe we forget that we don't experience true joy on a smooth celestial highway. To experience joy, we have to experience its opposite. Without opposition, sorrow, and pain, which act like the uphill climb on the roller coaster, there is no hill to descend, no thrill, no reward, no true joy.

Now, if you're still a little skeptical about this joy business, remember that after much serious research by learned scholars on the subject, scientists have discovered it's bad to suppress laughter. If you do, it sucks back down into your body and spreads out at your hips.

There are hundreds of ways to invite joy into family life without waiting until everything runs smoothly . . . because, frankly, it never will. Life gently tutors us *if* we remain open, vulnerable, and teachable. We don't grow without difficult challenges, truly love without risking rejection, or learn without making mistakes.

In kindergarten we were taught all about our five senses: touch, smell, sight, hearing, and taste. Well, there is an equally important sense they forgot to teach us. Our sixth sense is our sense of humor. Feeling joy by looking at life through humor-tinted lenses can be learned, practiced, and reinforced just like any other skill. Everyone has an innate sense of humor, but for most of us it's a tad dusty after years of neglect. Watch young children for a few minutes and see how easily they laugh. We can learn a great deal by observing our little ones and emulating their spontaneous light-heartedness.

I've found that humor is an effective way to manage the daily stress of family life and prevent parental burnout. Stress is actually caused by our perception of events, not the events themselves. We can't control what happens to us, but with a healthy dose of humor, we can control our perception of what happens to us. For instance, a well-known athlete was once being carried off the football field with a serious injury. This fellow had everything—money, fame, health—and now suddenly it was all threatened. Instead of caving in to despair, he quipped to the stretcher-bearers, "My mother was right. I'm *so* glad I have on clean underwear."

Research has determined that people who laugh frequently decrease their stress hormones and increase the body's defenses against diseases. People who are dour and gloomy exacerbate their illnesses and shorten their life spans. It's also a well-established fact that grouchy people are a pain to be around. Laughter is as important to our mental health as exercise is to our physical health. People should literally plan to be mirthful . . . at least five days a week for a minimum of twenty minutes a workout.

Also, to keep healthy we not only have to eat right but we have to think right. Mentally healthy people treat stress as a challenge or opportunity for growth rather than a negative event. Being able to laugh at ourselves—not to be confused with ridiculing other people—lifts our spirits. If we can find humor in something, especially ourselves, we can survive whatever comes our way.

Most family folklore includes experiences that didn't seem very funny at all when they happened. As a matter of fact, quite often catastrophe plus time equals humor. I remember a musical number our family performed in church a few years back. My husband was holding the baby and standing next to our children lined up in front of the pulpit. Right as I was about to begin the introduction on the piano, our toddler sucked the entire bulb section of the microphone into his mouth and blurted a long, protracted, "A-OOOOO-GA!" Every nodding member of the congregation suddenly woke with a jerk. My husband set the baby down so he could de-suction our toddler from the microphone, whereupon the baby immediately ran over to the piano and commenced banging on the keys. The younger children giggled uncontrollably; the older children were mortified to be part of this embarrassing family. Of course, I felt completely deflated. I'd been practicing with my family for months to get this number to a level that wouldn't detract from the spirit of the meeting . . . now this.

After the meeting was over, I received with surprise numerous kind comments that expressed one main thought, "That was the best musical number we've had in church for years." I can't remember if our family actually sang a note, but the congregation took the event in stride and couldn't wipe the smiles from their faces for the remainder of the meeting. I learned that day that other people don't expect families to be perfect. In fact, we are able to relate better with each other when we goof up.

Humor is not just telling jokes but looking at life and responding to it positively. When we decide to respond to life this way in spite of our circumstances, it's easier to find the silly or absurd around us. Take, for example, the church bulletin board notice announcing: "There will be meetings in the north and south ends of the church. Children will be baptized on both ends," or the sign on a hospital bulletin board: "Research shows that the first five minutes of life can be the most risky." Someone alert to absurdity had penciled underneath: "The last five minutes are pretty risky too." I like the label glued to a case containing a pair of women's glasses that reads: "If you have these, I don't. They are owned by a sweet little old lady who is driving home somewhere among your loved ones. Please return." Or the bumper sticker that reported: "If you actually look like your driver's license photo, you are not well enough to travel."

Once while I knelt with my three-year-old daughter, Ashley, as she said her bedtime prayers, she suddenly and without my prompting told her Heavenly Father a knock-knock joke. She even waited for him to answer and smiled when he apparently did so. After her amen, I must have looked a little stunned, for she seemed to see the need to relieve my apprehension, saying, "Don't worry, Mom. Heavenly Father likes to laugh sometimes, you know."

Humor is also a kissing cousin to creativity. When we

develop our sense of humor, we also increase our ability to tap our creative problem-solving abilities with our families. We can use humor to break the conflict cycle and find solutions to everyday problems. One wife found that if she clutched her heart and threw herself on the floor yelling, "Oh, you're so right it's killing me!" when she and her husband started arguing, the steam magically left the conflict. Because they were both being dramatic anyway, deciding to play the scene to the hilt wasn't just silly or funny, it was therapeutic.

Another reason to raise a family with a sense of humor is so that we can move from "grin and bear it" to "grin and share it." Take, for example, the classified advertisement stating: "Husband for sale, cheap. Comes complete with hunting and fishing equipment, one pair of jeans, two shirts, books, black Labrador retriever, and too many pounds of venison. Pretty good guy, but not home much from April to December. Will consider trade." After approximately sixty-six telephone calls, some of them serious, the wife placed another ad: "Retraction of husband for sale cheap. Everybody wants the dog, not the husband."

We can create our own joy simply by smiling even when we don't feel like it. Generally we don't laugh because we're happy; we're happy because we laugh. When we smile, we feel more relaxed. When we relax, a feeling of well-being comes over us. Smiling creates light from the inside.

Humor's lenses allow us not only to see what's funny

around us but to deflate a few of life's very real troubles. One concentration camp survivor advised her daughter: "Take life lightly. . . . Pain is inevitable, but suffering is optional." That is a profound thought. I admit it isn't always easy to reverse a bad mood, dark thoughts, or the evil choices of others. But we can change the way we feel by changing the way we think. I like to start that mental process by finishing this thought: "I'm so grateful for . . ." Grateful people are happy people. Joy comes when we're paying greater attention to all the things we're grateful for instead of all our problems.

Let me illustrate. I once knew a woman who was confined to bed because of a stroke at the same time I was in bed because of premature labor, and we became telephone buddies. Before her bed confinement, my friend Blanche had been confined to a wheelchair for thirty years because of a doctor's drunken mistake on the surgery table. After she returned home from the surgery, her husband left her. This woman raised four children alone in her wheelchair. She had every reason to focus on what she'd lost. Instead, she *chose* to focus on what she'd gained.

Blanche had one window in her bedroom from which she could see a single tree. During our telephone conversations, she would describe in intimate detail the intricate changes the seasons brought to her tree. "It's such a miracle to see," Blanche said. "I have so much to live for. I am so grateful I can see."

This dear lady used the same detailed descriptions when she spoke of her grandchildren. She saw beauty and blessings everywhere she looked because she *chose* to see with a grateful heart, even when her entire landscape was limited to a tiny bedroom. If I had been this woman, I'd have been a tad upset that I couldn't walk or get out of bed. But Blanche knew that the only true power we possess is our ability to see life as it really is. And life as it really is . . . is downright amazing.

Blanche also understood the value of creating our own celebrations. She often called me to wish me a "Happy Thursday at 2:15" or some such thing. She didn't wait for holidays or birthdays to celebrate or share her love of life. She understood that we have to be in charge of our own joy, for life is short.

Perhaps the greatest personal revelation I ever received was the day it dawned on me that if today wasn't the best day of my life, I'd never get to have the best day of my life. Can you imagine that—going through your whole life only to realize on your deathbed that you had a lousy time? If we continually look backward or forward for the good times, the good times never roll. In the end, I am the only one who can give my children a happy mother who loves life.

One major complaint of teens today is that their parents are boring. They may be right. I am at present the mother of many teens. I just wish my life were boring. Quite often I *try* to be boring just to even things out around my house. But what I think our adolescent children long for from us is playfulness. What we often give them instead is an acute case of hardening of the attitudes. We fail to truly look into their eyes and be touched by them, to see what wonderful individuals they are. We fail to open our hearts to them, to be vulnerable, to learn what they have to teach us, and to play with them.

Every season of family life is filled with good times and bad times, but we only get to live each time once, and then it's gone. Whether we're new parents coping with insomniac infants or hearing-impaired parents of stereo-blasting teens, each season cries out for and deserves our attention, regard, and appreciation.

Children of all ages are such great teachers. They live in the present and take spontaneous delight in today. Watch a small child for an hour and count how many times he laughs, cries, or giggles. When Christ told us to become as little children, I think that included emulating their obvious delight and enjoyment of life and their spontaneous ability to find a good laugh or cry in almost every situation.

As adults we often live life in the driver's seat by continually gazing in the rearview mirror. The space and time we see in that mirror has already been traveled through. We need to glance into the past occasionally, but we'll crash if we leave our eyes there. Our heavenly parents see all of us in the past, present, and future all at the same time. They see us whole, not in part, not blind to eternal progress. Because we lack the ability to see ourselves or others this way, we tend to make poor judgments about our potential and the potential of others. That's why we're told to leave the judging up to the One who truly sees.

Looking back, I think the reason I've chosen to write humorous family-life newspaper columns, magazine articles, and books is because I always heard from older, experienced parents that they didn't take the time to truly enjoy the years when they had their children at home; they didn't play enough or laugh enough. In order to write about the embarrassing, silly, or heartwarming things that happened to my family, I had to be able to notice, feel, and record all those moments. I couldn't let them slip past me unnoticed or unappreciated. Looking for the humor gave me a way to broaden my perspective, to see and feel more deeply the matters of the heart.

The scriptures tell us that if we "search diligently, pray always, and be believing, . . . *all* things shall work together for [our] good" (D&C 90:24; emphasis added). How do we begin to believe that? All things shall work together for our good? Even the awful things that happen to us or our children? I think we begin to believe first by changing our mind-set. We do this by becoming "inverse paranoids"—people who sincerely believe that common, everyday events are out there to do us good, to add to our experience and ultimate joy. If someone cuts in front of us on the freeway, we assume he is hurrying home with a dozen red roses for his wife and he just got so excited that his accelerator foot got stuck. We consistently practice assuming the best about people and situations.

We don't have nearly as much time as we think. This life is a gift, a fragile gift. Time flutters past us like a leaf in the wind, here one minute and gone on the next breeze. Our present family life is a gift—each stage passes so quickly that we have no time to put off living and loving. The reality of family life, today, gives us all the opportunity to learn truth through pain and gladness.

Religious people often judge themselves too harshly and see nothing humorous in their lives. That alone is pretty funny, for true religion is all about hope, forgiveness, love, and joy. We tend to forget that. I have been known to shake my finger at my children while insisting, "Quit laughing. This is not funny." If we would stop taking ourselves so seriously, we could grant ourselves and our children the healing gift of perspective. The core of the gospel of Jesus Christ, the Atonement, gives us all hope and an eternally joyous perspective. Our heavenly parents love us very much and want us to be happy. They know that life isn't easy; it wasn't meant to be. Life is hard. But once we accept the fact that life is difficult, a series of problems to face and work through, it ceases to be so hard.

Our heavenly parents want us to find joy in life, to share laughter and make human connections. They want us to accept life as it is and embrace it—to live fully and intimately.

Each of us will experience pain, heartache, and hills in our life that we'll doubt our ability to climb. But there is an unequaled joy awaiting if we can let go of the notion that we are in control of all those circumstances and relationships. Agency is a sacred thing, but the only real control we have is in how we accept and live with the present circumstances of our lives, how we choose to love and serve those around us. Our attitude ultimately becomes our character.

The power for positive change is not outside us but within us. It's not easy to find happiness in ourselves, but it's impossible to find it anywhere else. So let's not put off living and loving. Let's eat more ice cream, go barefoot more often, watch more sunsets, laugh more, cry more . . . feel more. Life is to be lived as we go along. It is the hills and valleys that make it a thrill.

These days, when I go to church with my own frazzled family, the newlywed behind me has to zip up my dress. Several of my children look like someone tossed them in the dryer without a static control sheet, and the baby is drooling copiously on his father's shoulder. I sigh and take it all in stride because I understand that if you keep both feet on the ground, you can't get your pants on . . . and it's even harder to dance.

Chapter Two

What the Experts Don't Tell You

Whatever the season, the best way to survive parenthood is

to quit listening to the experts and have yourself declared

legally insane—at least until the kids are grown and have to

accept full responsibility for their own behavior. Truth is, no

matter how hard we try, we never feel we can compete with

the sainted, machine-processed, greeting-card image of parenthood. Maternal and paternal pedestals are dangerous places. Most parents I know would rather take a flying leap off a cliff than deal with the loneliness and lack of oxygen up on those lofty heights.

When I was twenty-two years old, I celebrated my first Mother's Day as the terrified, brand-new mother of a three-week-old premature baby with jaundice. I'll never forget standing in church to receive my very first Mother's Day potted plant. I took that healthy, thriving plant home and promptly murdered it. Panicked, I was certain that the deader-than-a-doornail plant was a barometer of my mothering abilities.

I still can't believe that my first baby survived my perfectionist craziness. Back then, I had the foolish notion that real mothers were saints or angels. I've since learned that angels and saints are just people who take themselves lightly. So should parents. I heard a pregnant mother say in church one Mother's Day, "All you old ladies always say you're glad you're not raising your children today. You say the world is so awful. Well, I want you to stop it. You're scaring me to death."

"Don't worry, dear," an elderly lady answered, patting the young pregnant woman on the shoulder. "My grandmother used to say the same thing to me fifty years ago."

Maternal and paternal job descriptions change so fast, it's hard to keep up. We stretch ourselves so far that we think we'll explode, but we generally wind up growing instead. Family making is tough, but it is the most rewarding thing any of us will ever do with our lives.

When you're a first-time expectant parent, mothers and fathers who have been through childbirth love to recite their most horrific stories of marathon labors to scare you to death. When you're a walking zombie trying desperately to soothe a newborn, more experienced parents tend to say things like, "They're only babies once. Just enjoy them, dear." When you're on the brink of a nervous breakdown with a house full of insomniac terrorist toddlers down with chicken pox, older parents say, "Just wait till you have teenagers. You ain't seen nothing yet." When you're battling fire-breathing teenagers, older parents say, "Don't wait for the children to leave home before you get a life, because . . . *they come back!*"

Younger parents think their older peers have grown senile and forgotten the bad parts. Older parents think their younger peers will soon regret not having enjoyed their children while they still had them home to tuck into bed each night. The unwritten code of maternal and paternal martyrdom states, "All *other* parents must have it easier than I do, because if I really believed things were going to get worse, I wouldn't get out of bed." If we really knew what was ahead, we'd probably avoid making the very choices that ultimately bring us the most joy. Family life doesn't get easier as we go along, it just gets different. In truth, older parents look back at younger parents with a certain tenderness only experience can bestow. We need each other, for the parenthood trek is not for weenies.

It seemed like every time I got pregnant, I read about some new-age woman dressed in color-coordinated leotards who jogged to the hospital—in active labor, mind you—to deliver her baby. I myself was never a heroic pregnant lady. I conquered no new ground, scaled no new heights. My single goal in life, as delivery day approached, was to find a place to sit down.

When I was pregnant, people constantly stared at me when I went out in public . . . and it wasn't my face they were looking at. I'm not a tall, stately female. I'm short with no place to hide unborn babies, so they poke straight out front. Way too many people laughed at my appearance, as if I were deliberately trying to be funny or something. Total strangers asked me if I had swallowed a basketball. My children called me the beached whale. I was always astounded that my body could stretch that far without exploding. I tried not to waddle, but when you're shifting that much weight with every step, it's downright impossible to avoid.

I never could keep my pantyhose up over my pregnant figure. It was awfully annoying, not to mention embarrassing, to feel the sudden need to grab my slipping waistband as my pantyhose fell down around my knees. Clothing that had once draped nicely over my body became impossible to stretch around the new, gigantic me. Before long, nothing fit anymore, not even the one-size-fits-all tents they sell at maternity shops. I kept telling the doctor I must be holding water. (Frankly, that was just an excuse I gave so I wouldn't get the "you're gaining too much weight" lecture. Never worked.)

The one benefit of pregnancy was that my body temperature rose until I was toasty warm in the winter. The drawback was that in the summer I was always trying to figure out what article of clothing I could discreetly take off in public without being arrested.

The last month of pregnancy was designed so that women would be willing to go through with labor and delivery just to get it over with. We get so miserable to live with, our husbands are willing to go through anything to get it over with too.

But despite all my complaining, I have to admit that taking part in the creation of another human being has been the closest I've ever come to a partnership with God. Feeling a tiny someone grow, stretch, and move inside me is an honest-to-goodness, one-of-a-kind wonder. Even during the last few weeks, I knew it was worth it. Babies are life's greatest miracles. There is no thrill that comes close to holding a brand-new person in your arms for the first time.

Getting the little darling to go to sleep after he or she arrives, now, that's another story. Soothing that little bundle to sleep has forced exhausted parents the world over into bizarre behavior for thousands of years.

"Is she asleep yet?" burned-out father whispers to frazzled mother as he waltzes across living-room floor with baby one more time. "I can't see her eyes."

"They're rolling," exhausted mother whispers back. "Eyelids at half-mast and lowering fast. Hang in there. I think you've almost got her."

All worn-out parents know that babies come in two categories: sleepers and nonsleepers. Sleepers are the ones who purr on your shoulder at church, nod off in their car seats, doze on the handlebar of the grocery-store cart, and snooze all night in their cribs. Nonsleepers, on the other hand, howl at church, dismantle their car seats with screwdrivers they have hidden in their diapers, pitch every breakable object on the floor at the grocery store, and play "I'm Awake Again!" all night in their cribs.

Parents of nonsleepers have been known to crawl across the bedroom floor on their elbows at 2:06 A.M., mumbling a prayer that they will not make the slightest sound and wake baby again. Siblings of nonsleepers are frequently threatened, "I have been up with that baby all night, and if you make even the tiniest sound and wake her, I will personally see to it that you are shot at sunrise." Nonsleepers love to fake drowsiness while their parents pat them on the back and make soothing go-to-sleep sounds. If a parent breaks the "there-there" pattern by trying to slow down or skip a pat, nonsleepers will immediately zap open their eyelids, stare at the beleaguered parent, and totally disintegrate into sobs.

Parents of a nonsleeper develop great juggling talents. Because their child never sleeps, Mom and Dad learn to type, peel potatoes, talk on the telephone, trim their toenails, play the piano, and take showers—all with a tiny, wide-eyed body glued to their chest or hip. Parents of sleepers frequently throw parents of nonsleepers into great pits of depression as they brag about how long their babies snooze at night or how much work they get done during the day while their little sweethearts nap.

Parents of a sleeper like to take Junior along everywhere they go because he always rests peacefully in his stroller, attracting comments from strangers like, "Oh, what a little cutie." "Don't you just love babies?" "Would you look at that angel!" Parents of nonsleepers will do anything for a break. Baby-sitters suddenly become the most coveted prize in the neighborhood. If all else fails, and Mom and Dad are forced to take Junior along, they learn to ignore glares from strangers and unsolicited suggestions about how to stop their baby from screaming.

You can spot the parents of a nonsleeper a mile off. Bloodshot eyes, Don King hair, one hip lower than the other, and a constant swaying motion give them away every time.

To parents of nonsleepers I say, Do not despair. Nonsleepers grow up. They become teenagers who want to party all night and play their stereos so loud that the hair on the back of your neck sticks straight out.

First-time mothers and fathers, be warned: nonsleepers are not the only individuals out there with the single goal of driving new parents daffy. I've been in the baby business for over two decades, and I'm here to tell you that so-called experts will mess with your mind big time. If you listen to what every authority figure says, you'll go crazy, because experts keep changing their minds.

For instance, when I started having children over twenty years ago, I was completely amazed at how intelligent my babies were. All the doctors and nurses were telling me that my infant couldn't really see, let alone smile during those first weeks. But my extremely bright babies were obviously doing both. According to the experts, this was just gas, and I would soon get over my easily astonished nature. Well, the experts were wrong. Watching my babies grow and develop in those early weeks and subsequent years continued to be a source of continual amazement.

Then, when my youngest turned three, the experts changed their minds. They told me I'd already missed my chance to "maximize her intellectual growth." According to them, a child's environment influences the number of brain cells the child keeps and the connections between them. These experts say the brain is literally shaped by experience. Sensory experiences can affect which brain cells live or die. According to these guys, babies are born with billions of brain cells, twice as many as adults. During the first few months of life, bridges or connections between the brain's cells, otherwise known as synapses, multiply rapidly to a thousand trillion, making the structures that allow learning to happen. Don't ask me how they counted them.

I think these scientists could save themselves a lot of trouble by just interviewing, say, a dozen parents of real babies. The researchers could ask such intelligent questions as, "Is your baby smart?"

"Are you kidding?" a parent would answer. "This child knows the exact moment I lay my head on the pillow, even when he is in the other room. If you ask me, my baby has about a thousand trillion brain cells."

Negative experiences in early childhood can have lasting effects, the experts also say, because they can alter the organization of the brain. On the other hand, these experts say, parents should not get paranoid about the new research and become overzealous about stimulating their children's brains with flash cards in the delivery room or lullabies incorporating all the elements in the periodic table.

The experts seem to forget that we parents are not stupid. We are tired, but we are not stupid. We parents know who runs the household . . . and the world. The under-three set pretty much rules the roost. The reason it takes the scientists so long to figure all this out is because, just like they said, the scientists have only half as many brain cells as the babies.

Don't even think about listening to the experts when it comes to the next essential rite of passage for all parents of young children. If all the dedicated parents I know were asked to sit down and list their three *least* favorite duties of parenthood, I think they'd unanimously write:

1. toilet training,
2. toilet training, and
3. toilet training.

Boot-camp patrol to enforce your child's move from disposable pants to training pants is no laughing matter. With my first child, I was so excited to show her the joys of a diaperless existence, I started potty patrol before the poor child's second birthday. I made such a big deal out of my toddler's maturity for wearing training pants, she went right along with things and refused to wear a diaper even when I later regretted my ill-informed and hasty decision. I later found myself longing for those good old diaper days.

The older I get, the more I'm starting to see things from my child's point of view. Just imagine for a minute that you're a very small person—so small, in fact, that your feet never touch the floor when you're seated anywhere. Now imagine that a very large, serious person, three or four times your size, suddenly picks you up, exposes your privacy, plops you on a large, white, gaping porcelain hole, and tells you to relax. I mean, you're no dummy. You've watched that hole before and you're well aware that everything that falls inside suddenly disappears when you pull down on a little silver knob. The way I see it, young children are amazingly patient with their inexperienced parents' attempts to eliminate diaper duty.

By the time I'd trained a half-dozen children, I finally learned not to worry about it so much. My later children had to make me wild promises before I'd let them train themselves. If my child has the basic idea before he leaves home, that's fine with me. I mean, why rush things and ruin your life? I've learned there are worse things than changing a diaper, like making a wild swooping leap for the bathroom every time your toddler gets a concerned look on his face, shampooing the entire living-room carpet every week, or washing forty-seven batches of damp laundry a day.

Things would definitely be much easier if children came housebroken and fully equipped to handle their own bathroom emergencies. But life with children wasn't designed to be easy. Life on Planet Parenthood takes daring, skill, and a heck of a lot of wet wipes. Parenting young children is—to put it mildly—exhausting. But if you're a parent of young children, don't despair; this too will pass. Don't let the experts intimidate you by dictating when.

Parenting authorities are constantly telling us to understand our children. But how do you understand someone who will rummage through garbage cans for used gum and then turn around and refuse to give you a kiss because there's spit on your lips? How do you understand someone who climbs to the top of the swing set and effortlessly impersonates a circus tightrope performer with perfect balance, then later finds it impossible to walk to his bedroom without sliding his greasy hands down both walls in the hallway for support? Why does the same child who just played a rousing game of tag with the neighbors insist he's abused if his parent doesn't give him a ride to basketball practice two blocks away? It's no wonder parents lose their marbles and start calling their children, "Ap, Aub, Jor, Jo, oh, whoever-you-are, get in here!" It's no wonder parents lie awake at night worrying about what will become of their children if the parents die and there is no one left who knows how to replace the toilet-paper roll. This is territory the experts have yet to conquer.

Finally, experts report that camping, of all things, is the most common activity of happy families. The Baadsgaards go camping quite a bit, but, just between you and me, I'm not a happy camper. My idea of a good time always includes lots of toilet paper and clean sheets. Even I must admit, however, that there's something about camping that brings out the best as well as the worst in families. Venturing into "them there hills" takes nerves of steel, especially if you decide to take children along.

A while back, my husband and I took our family to a campground we hadn't frequented since we were newly married. The first time we camped there, we romantically roasted marshmallows in this pine-forested area up Payson Canyon and survived for days with one tiny sack of groceries. Since our family statistics and food allowance have exploded, this time we had to hire a U-Haul trailer to pack enough food up the canyon for several meals. I had visions of happy children running through the woods discovering the beauties of creation. What I got was a mud flood because my two young sons decided to play with the water tap above the camp. I had visions of contented children singing around the campfire. What I got was an assortment of adolescents conducting a spitting contest into the fire to see who could make the most smoke. I had visions of my happy children enjoying God's magnificent creations: breathing fresh mountain air, dipping their toes in clear mountain streams, running with majestic deer, and smelling the wildflowers. What I got was several kids who could hike roughly two micro-inches before blurting out, "I'm hungry! I'm tired! I have to go to the bathroom!" And let me tell you, there's nothing quite like eating burned tinfoil dinners off a sticky, fly-infested picnic table because you forgot the charcoal and the tablecloth.

Twenty-six loads of laundry and eighty-seven bug bites later, we packed up the troops and supplies and headed back down the canyon. "How would you rate this little family outing on a scale of one to ten?" my husband grinned across the car seat, with several smelly children between us. Before I had a chance to answer, several fire-blackened, insect-bitten children yelled from the backseat, "Ten!"

That's what's so weird about camping. You get dirty and

smelly but you find yourself smiling all the way home. Your children pack back slimy snail shells by the dozens and several hundred pounds of rocks, leaves, and sticks, but you're glad you came. You find yourself singing dumb camp songs at the top of your lungs with a motley crew you've recently relearned to love. Don't ask me why we regularly throw away running water, modern appliances, and indoor plumbing for this annual primeval ritual. I think maybe it's a modern curiosity to see what our children will do when they aren't plugged into the nearest television, computer, or Nintendo. Yes, camping remains the most common activity of happy families, according to the experts. What the experts don't tell you is that those families are happy because they're so glad to be back home. Home never looked so good.

Chapter Three

New Parental Styles for the Children-Impaired

My sense of style has definitely changed since I became a

mother. I used to go for the conventional, traditional, and

stately look in clothing, furniture, and transportation. Now

I go for comfort, wash-and-wear, and the ability to hide

spots.

When my husband and I picked out carpet in our childless days, we shopped for flooring that was elegant but understated. Our nine children have changed our selection process dramatically. The other day, my husband and I were in the store browsing through carpet samples. Our conversation went something like this:

"Hey, Jan, how about this one?"

"Too light. It will show the dark dirt."

"How about this one?"

"Too dark. It will show the light dirt."

"How about this one?"

"It would show bloodstains."

"This one?"

"It would show mud stains."

We finally picked out a gray carpet with multicolored flecks, upon which the kids could grow science experiments, sponsor mustard-squirting contests, slop spaghetti, dump red fruit punch, and track in mud from the compost heap and you'd never notice.

I used to dream of decorating my house with elegant furniture straight from the Ethan Allen catalogue. Words like *heirloom, country French, mahogany,* and *craftsmanship* actually crossed my lips. Now I select furniture based on whether the fabric and wood tones will survive the children's ballpoint-pen masterpieces.

During my single days, I used to buy clothing designed to give me an air of distinction. Now I won't buy anything without an elastic waistband and wash-and-wear laundry instructions. If my babies can't drool on my shoulder pad without a hefty dry-cleaning bill to pay, it's just not my style. There are simply some things more important to me than appearances these days.

I used to dream of owning a car with a flawless white paint job and a burgundy velvet interior. Now I select my transportation based on the number of installed seat belts and how much it will cost me to insure it with multiple teenage drivers in the family. Rust spots, paint scratches, and dents that someone else has inflicted on the used automobile I shop for today will soon blend in with the spots, scratches, and dents my children will inflict after I buy it. When you drive a clunker, you don't have to blow a gasket when your sixteen-year-old plows it into the back of a cement truck and puts the poor thing out of its misery (the car, not the teenager).

All in all, having children tends to help parents develop a much more subtle sense of style and decorum. Gum stuck to the seat of your pants, oatmeal stains splattered on your tie, and melted red crayon splotches on your underwear tend to keep your set of values in check. After all, what good is it to have a dent-free car, stylish clothes, and unstained carpet if you don't have any soft, chubby, bright faces screaming through the house, hanging on your leg, or reaching up for a big, juicy kiss? After many years of marriage and many children, I think my sense of style has improved immensely.

Yes, your perspective changes as you gain more experience as a parent. For example, for the first few years of your parenting career, you spend untold hours coaxing your children to talk and walk. Then you spend the rest of your life trying to get them to sit down and hush up. It's not that we parents don't love our children. It's just that there are times occasionally when we crave that rare moment of peace and quiet. Even normally patient parents sometimes find themselves yelling, "I don't care whose fault it is. If there's no blood, I don't want to hear about it!"

It is difficult to ad-lib an adequately intimidating yet believable parental threat to get children to quit fighting. Intimidation is serious business for parents, and I've never been very good at it. When I summon the hordes to supper by yelling, "Come and get it or I'll throw it out," no one moves even one microscopic muscle cell. So I resort to following telephone cords around corners, under doors, and into closets, where I hear whispered voices saying, "Shhh. I think she's listening. I have to hang up now." Then I proceed to unplug headphones and televisions. Next comes the daily train ride through the yard, where I pull unwilling children off bicycles, swings, and the neighbor boy's head.

If being an intimidating parent is difficult at home, it is impossible at the playground. You find yourself shouting comments like, "You get down from there! Do you hear me?

Get down from there this instant, before you fall and break your neck! All right, young man, when you're dead, don't come running to me for sympathy." I'm just not the take-charge mom I used to be.

I also think I'm regressing in my imparting of good table manners to my posterity. I used to focus on things like keeping elbows off the table and saying "please" and "thank you." Now my rules are more along the lines of: "All family members are required to leave at least one foot on the floor at all times during the meal," or "Food bombing is not allowed."

The combination of food and children has a way of bringing out the mess mania in families. My children often ask my husband and me if we wouldn't like to go on a date or a walk together so they can splatter cheese in the microwave and break the tips off all our knives trying to open tin cans filled with mandarin oranges. While I've been distracted, my children have slashed my kitchen chairs with butcher knives, gnawed through china plates and cups, and filled all my empty fruit jars with black-widow spiders, potato bugs, and slugs. The other day when I wanted a drink of water, I had to use my toddler's training cup because every other glass in the house was under the children's beds, out in the sandbox, or sitting, dirty, in the kitchen sink. Mind you, this was merely two hours after I had unloaded all the clean glasses in the house from the dishwasher into the cupboard.

Cooking for a family is another thankless task, because every time you do it, the family eats it. You can spend hours creating a meal that takes about sixty-three seconds to work its way into the digestive tracts of your offspring.

Speaking of cooking, I've noticed that the migratory path of leftovers through my refrigerator has changed dramatically over the years. As a young bride, I found myself overrun with volcanic mountains of leftover macaroni salad because I was so accustomed to cooking for an army. Being raised in a family of eleven had taught me to cook . . . a lot. So my poor new husband ate what I cooked on Monday for the rest of the week.

Just when I had grown accustomed to cooking for a twosome, we became a threesome, then a foursome, and on and on to the elevensome we are today. These days my husband and I haul in apples and oranges by the bushel and gallons of milk by the dozen. We've discussed buying dried dog food in those king-sized packages and debated over whether the children would notice the substitution at the breakfast table. We've grown accustomed to people dropping their mouths and staring at our grocery cart in the supermarket. There was a time when I could make a cake and serve it twice. There was a time when I could make a huge pot of soup and have enough left over for lunch the next day. If you open my refrigerator these days, you'll find one empty plastic milk container, an old glass jar filled with turkey fat left over from Thanksgiving, half a bottle of soy sauce, and a dead celery leaf in the crisper.

"Why don't we ever have anything to eat around here!" my son bellows after his 100-yard dash to the fridge after school.

"Because you ate it already," I answer. "If you kids would quit eating, we'd have a lot more food around here."

The only food that has hung around for longer than a microsecond at our house in the last ten years was a batch of peanut butter cookies I made with four cups of salt instead of sugar. (Come to think of it, we went through a lot of milk and water about the same time.)

"You used to cook more," my daughter lamented the other day. "Remember the homemade bread you used to make all the time?"

"That was before you kids could scarf down one loaf apiece in one sitting," I answered. It's not that I'm complaining or anything like that, but life would be so much easier for parents if humans didn't require feeding. Think about all the spare time we'd have if we didn't have to earn money for food, shop for food, grow food, store food, prepare food, bottle food, clean up after food, and dispose of food.

If you really want to feel paranoid about children and food, consider this: In a child-development class I attended at the university a few years ago, the instructor told us he once did home evaluations for a social-service organization. Whenever he arrived for a home visit, the carpet pile was always standing straight up, and so was the family. It was difficult to get the family members to relax and act natural. So this man had devised a sneaky way to see the people he was evaluating in a more natural light. What did he do? He asked to eat a meal with them. For some reason, chowing down at the family feeding trough tends to break down false fronts, and people begin acting like their normal selves.

I sat behind my desk listening to this professor with my mouth open. You see, I could well remember my family's most recent meal together. The idea that my family could be evaluated based on our mealtime habits made me a bit paranoid. How would my yelling at the kids to stop launching their meatballs show up on a clinical evaluation? I couldn't take the biggest piece of cake without worrying about what secret neglect my behavior revealed. I couldn't stare into space with cotton balls in my ears during the meal without worrying about how that kind of behavior would affect my children for generations to come.

And if my behavior was under scrutiny, what about my children's? I couldn't watch them eat without wondering what weirdos they'd turn out to be. I just knew the three-year-old meat jabbers were going to turn out to be mass murderers, and the eternal milk spillers would wander through life clueless and unaware.

After a while, I decided to have a little more fun with the idea of personality profiles drawn from the dinner table. For instance, we took the tribe to a buffet-style family restaurant the other day, and boy, was that ever an eye-opener! With an entire full-course meal buffet to choose from, my six-year-old selected thirteen glasses of fruit punch and a pile of raisins that roughly resembled Mount Fuji. Was this child being deprived at home?

My two-year-old licked everything on her plate but didn't actually eat anything. Was this child being overindulged at home? My teenagers laughed when I brought a brownie, frozen chocolate yogurt smothered with chocolate sauce, and a cup of chocolate pudding back to the table. Was this the clue to the size of my poochy stomach?

Some family members went right for the main course, and some ate their fruit and vegetables first. I worried if the dessert-first kids would have a hard time holding down jobs and completing their college educations. Then I worried if the vegetable-first kids would lack spontaneity and fun in life.

But mostly I worried about the most important issue this whole silly family-meal business produced: finding a bathroom, pronto, for the six-year-old who just finished off his thirteenth glass of fruit punch.

Analysis aside, there's something about looking around the table at your wild, wonderful, crazy family throwing food, reaching over each other, burping without saying excuse me, and spilling their milk that gets to you right where it counts and tells you that someday, too soon, your family mealtimes will be peaceful and boring.

So when I find myself sitting alone at the messy kitchen table after everyone else has abandoned ship after supper and left me with the dishes again, I say, in more ways than one, "Amen."

Chapter Four

Dreams Just Aren't What They Used to Be

Dreams of having the perfect family often change while

you're actually raising one. Real-estate salesmen dream of

the big sale. Lawyers dream of the big case. Parents dream

of being able to find something where they left it. I have a garden-hose nozzle hidden behind the cosmetic mirror in my bathroom. I know it's only a matter of days before the kids find my latest hiding place, but it's comforting to know I can find my favorite weapon for at least a few more days. Some child is always carrying off everything I own, including my comb and brush, toothbrush, toilet paper, car keys, sense of humor, and privacy. It's enough to drive a mother to hide her garden-hose nozzle behind her makeup mirror.

Farmers dream of a bumper cash crop. Politicians dream of a huge tax increase. Taxpayers dream of a huge tax cut. Parents dream of walking across the kitchen floor without sticking to something. I think my children will remember me as the hovering angel of washragness. Refrigerator handles, telephone receivers, doorknobs, bathroom fixtures, sliding glass doors, and every other surface in my home seems constantly covered with child marks. No matter how hard I try to keep things wiped up, there's always a gob of grape jam or applesauce or some other unidentifiable goo lurking around the corner, waiting for my naked foot.

Contractors dream of the completed home. Firefighters dream of the rescued child. Parents dream of going to the bathroom without an audience. The last time I had any privacy in the bathroom was about twenty years ago when I was newly married and my husband was in class at BYU. When you have babies, they always start crying just as you step in the shower, but they tend to calm down if you bring them into the bathroom with you and entertain them. I've taken many a bath while tap dancing and singing, "I'm singing in the shower, Oh, singing in the shower!" to entertain a fussy baby.

Toddlers like to follow you into the bathroom and ask short, blunt questions. School-age children tend to unseat you with desperate pleas. They always wait until the last moment before they dash into the bathroom, red-faced and urgent. When you have teens, you have to stand in line for hours studying the paint job in the hall while you wait for someone to shower, blow dry, curl, crimp, make-up, deodorize, and perfume.

Authors dream of hitting the best-seller list. Teachers dream of summer vacation. Parents dream of eating one meal without leaping up to catch a glass of red punch flying through the air. I don't know about you, but mealtimes around our house are not restful. Mothers don't need diets. They just need someone to invite them out for dinner.

Ministers dream of a large, adoring congregation. Postal workers dream of an end to junk mail. Parents dream of actually sleeping at night. If you have babies, you're up at all hours of the night rocking, hugging, and comforting. If you have teens, you're up waiting for them to get home from dates. If you have babies *and* teens—sleep is only a memory.

My dreams have been taking on a major transformation lately. I used to dream of a nice house, two cars, and foreign travel. Now that I'm a mother of nine, my ultimate dream is to take a nap.

Children have a way of forcing parents to rearrange their priorities. Keeping up appearances, for example, is a lost cause. Pity the parent who must host houseguests while raising a family. The dream of hospitality quickly becomes a nightmare. How do you put your best foot forward when your audience can see your naked toes, warts and all?

Suppose I have a family of seven coming to stay at my house. This means there will soon be eighteen people lurking about, staring at me in my ratty nightgown, accidentally walking in on me when I'm in the bathroom, and staring into my empty refrigerator searching for something edible.

Making plans for houseguests tends to make mothers downright paranoid. Contemplating the various sleeping arrangements for my houseguests always gives me the hives. The only place to sleep a man and wife is in my nine- and ten-year-old sons' bedroom. If you've never had or been a ten-year-old boy, you can't possibly understand the nightmare this arrangement brings to mind. Boys this age love to collect rocks they've cracked open in their sheets, and to hide creepy creatures under their beds along with their dirty socks, week-old gum, broken kites, unfinished homework, candy wrappers, and pizza bones. The walls in my boys' bedroom are plastered with large, imposing posters of sweaty basketball stars in various tongue-hanging maneuvers, movie characters, *National Geographic* wildlife enlargements, and handwritten warnings that read "Enter this room uninvited and die!" "This is our room so keep out you jughead!"

Another major problem with hosting houseguests is my sudden attack of medicine-cabinet paranoia. The thought of someone opening my bathroom cabinet and learning my deepest, darkest secrets is unnerving, to say the least. If you can't hide your intimate details in your own private medicine cabinet, what's a host to do?

Another challenge that comes with hosting houseguests is that you can't get your resident family to quit living in your house and cluttering it up while you're tying to get things ready. Family members tend to believe they can just keep eating, sleeping, and making a mess in their own house as if no one were coming to stay at all. I find myself wanting to move my own family in with the neighbors for a few days so the house will stay clean until the guests arrive.

My children are supposed to clean their own bedrooms and bathrooms. Most of the time I've learned to live with their efforts by closing the door and pretending. But when houseguests are on their way, the rules change, and I find myself following up on my children's cleaning efforts with a keen eye for dead flies, cobwebs, and dirty underwear. My children don't throw away old frayed toothbrushes, they collect them. They love to decorate our bathroom mirrors with blue cement toothpaste murals.

Just before my houseguests arrive, my bathroom towels suddenly don't seem good enough anymore, and my dishes look scratched and chipped. I've cringed at the peeling paint around the shower stall and taken mental note of every stain on my carpet. My closets and cabinets, formerly great places to hide a bunch of junk, transform into potential inspection sites.

I think this problem must be universal. A while back when I was playing houseguest instead of host, I was warmly welcomed into my host's perfectly clean home. Even the carpet pile was still saluting.

Before I could even sit down, my young niece grabbed me around the neck and sighed, "Boy, am I glad you're finally here! We've been working our tails off for days trying to get this place cleaned up, and I'm exhausted."

My sister blushed. House-host phobia must be universal.

Dreams also change into nightmares when your children are under the weather. Sick children generally produce sick parents. For example, chicken pox is a common parental disease that regularly progresses through the following stages:

Paranoid Parent Stage I

During this stage, parents are on constant red alert for any possible sinister chicken-pox contamination in the area. At the first sign that another child in the neighborhood, school, church group, or day-care center has chicken pox, parents will wrap their children in sterile gauze and lock them in their bedrooms for the next seventeen years.

Paranoid Parent Stage II

During this stage, parents believe their child has been exposed to chicken pox, so they spend the next two or three decades checking for any suspicious red spots at bath time and mentally composing detailed death threats to the individual who exposed their child.

Paranoid Parent Stage III

During this stage, parents quit checking for any suspicious signs because bright red spots are now popping out so fast on their sick child that he roughly resembles a flashing red railroad-crossing warning signal. Parents try in vain to keep the sick child away from mirrors so he won't discover he can do dot-to-dot puzzles on his face.

Paranoid Parent Stage IV

During this stage, parents notice flat, red splotches turning into huge, disfiguring sores. The sick child suddenly turns into a twitching maniac who won't sleep or eat but has strong, uncontrollable urges to scratch off his entire epidermis. During this stage, parents cut fingernails, plead, bribe, and pray.

Paranoid Parent Stage V

During this stage, parents are willing to try anything just so they can sleep for a minute or two. The battle is on. Weapons include baking-soda baths, acetaminophen, and antihistamines. Even after the valiant struggle, dazed parents wave a white flag over the moon-crater battlefield on the tip of Junior's nose. During this stage, every parent knows for certain that this child will never want to go out in public again.

Paranoid Parent Stage VI

After several long weeks of sleepless nights and home confinement, most parents foolishly take a deep breath and relax during this last stage. Just when parents head for the easy chair, sibling number two comes down with the dreaded disease. Ninety percent of brothers and sisters will catch chicken pox from their infected sibling even if the parent makes a valiant attempt to isolate the sick child. If, however, a parent deliberately exposes the entire family to the virus just to get it over with, everybody will stay perfectly well until the night before their parents are booked to leave on a once-in-a-lifetime trip to Europe, or just in time to greet the new baby home from the hospital.

Doctors will tell you that chicken pox can be effectively treated at home. They will tell you this because they sure as heck don't want your germy child screaming in their waiting room. In normally healthy children, this ailment has few lasting ill effects, but in parents, chicken pox can be a devastating, life-altering disease.

If childhood diseases don't drive you crazy, your major appliances will. I used to dream of a house full of gleaming labor-saving devices. Now I dream to have one full day in which every single appliance we own is actually in working order.

I remember one early morning when our daughter

walked into our bedroom and announced, "Mom and Dad, it's raining in the basement!" We jumped out of bed and ran downstairs. The ceiling was bulging in some spots and collapsing onto the soaked carpet in others. We soon discovered that the dishwasher had malfunctioned during the night while we slept, flooding our home. Mornings are usually hectic at our house, but this dishwasher flood just wasn't funny. My nine offspring, ranging from preschoolers to university-age children, sloshed around the house trying desperately to get ready for school while my husband and I frantically soaked up water with every available towel. Next we dragged our entire two-year's supply of damp wheat and wet powdered milk from the soaked storage room to the sunny backyard. Just as we finally got the storage room empty, the sky darkened and it began to rain, forcing us to move our food storage into the garage.

Later that night, completely frustrated and exhausted, our soggy family of eleven surrounded the dinner table sharing the news of our collective bad luck that day. Besides the house flood, our university-age daughter had misplaced her car in the parking lot and was late for work. Our kindergarten-age daughter had had an accident at recess that required an immediate change of clothing. Our high-school-age daughter had broken her front tooth off playing powder-puff football. Our junior-high-age children had either missed the bus, forgotten band instruments, or left their clean gym clothes home. My husband had discovered that his good friend was depressed and getting a divorce, and I had realized that we had changed our homeowner's insurance policy from a $250 to a $500 deductible just three days before Noah's curse.

After listening for a while, my five-year-old blurted out loudly enough to be heard over the disagreeable din at the dinner table, "Mommy, couldn't Heavenly Father just put a rainbow over our house?"

We all turned, glared at her, and then burst into laughter that went on until tears were streaming. We realized that the dripping carpets, lost cars, broken teeth, and tight budgets weren't the end of the world. We still had each other and that was a happy reality that surpassed any fleeting dream of a perfect, problem-free life.

Here's another dream gone awry: The happy family garden plot. This April dream often degenerates into a September quest to find a place to unload all the extra stuff you grow and can't stand to eat anymore. People generally find out they have more zucchini and tomatoes than they have friends. Backyard gardeners sneak around leaving anonymous parcels of green war missiles on front doorsteps.

When I had a friend over the other day, I thought I might be able to unload some of my extra tomatoes so I wouldn't have to put them up.

"Please take some of these tomatoes," I said. "We have gobs more."

My friend hesitated, then reached down into the basket.

"Please, please, take more," I insisted.

My friend hesitated again but dutifully took a few more.

"Please, take all you want," I coaxed again.

My friend heaved a sigh of relief, carefully set all the tomatoes back in the basket, and walked home.

Garden season has a way of bringing out the ~~ulterior~~ spontaneous generosity in us. Friends and family I haven't heard from all summer are suddenly calling to offer raspberries, plums, peaches, squash, and a variety of other delicious items I don't have time to accept because I'm too busy calling my friends and family to take mine.

I've been told that it's mentally healthy to grow a garden and watch the miracle of nature transpire before your eyes. The planting, watering, weeding, and eventual harvesting can offer great parallels to life. I think a garden teaches other lessons as well.

I remember when my husband brought our first home-grown tomato into the house one summer. The children ohhhhhed and ahhhhhed. After eating tomatoes for breakfast, lunch, and dinner for the next several months, our kids just didn't get excited anymore when they saw another red beauty. Whenever we have too much of anything, the novelty wears thin and our appreciation evaporates.

Dreams of getting back in shape are another example of parental fantasy that often ends up on the editing-room floor. Every spring I decide I'm really going to do it, after a long winter of creative excuses about why I can't get out and exercise: "It's too cold." "I think I might be coming down with something." "I just hate it when my nose hair freezes." "If God had intended for human beings to act alive in the winter, he would have given us moose hair and skis for feet."

With springtime's warm weather, my excuses don't hold up. Even crabby bears have to come out of hibernation eventually, so I usually decide to hit the road. My plan is simple: I accompany my disciplined husband on his daily run.

On my first springtime run, my husband jogs alongside trying to keep me happy with pleasant conversation. Problem is, I can't run and talk at the same time because I have to use my mouth for gasping. Right about the time I think I'll drop dead from exhaustion, I make it to the end of our driveway, and my husband begins his stretching exercises.

The only stretching exercises I've done for the past twenty years have been from the body-expanding experience known as pregnancy.

"Now reach over and try to touch your toes," my husband says.

I reach over and touch my thighs.

"Well, on second thought, maybe you better try for the knees," my husband amends.

After my husband's stretching and my moaning, we begin the actual running stuff. I jog along beside my husband for roughly seven seconds before I take one last desperate gasp of air and slow to a walk.

"You go ahead," I say to Ross. "Don't let me slow you down."

My husband jogs ahead of me for about 26 miles. Then he jogs back to where I am limping along, then jogs ahead another 107 miles, then back. On one of his jog-bys, he gives me a sympathetic pat on the back.

I watch my husband jog ahead again. The sun is now going down in the western horizon, and I can see his tall, dark figure silhouetted against the amber sky as he reaches the crest of the hill and then disappears from view.

I spy a telephone pole ahead.

"I'll run to that telephone pole, and then I'll die," I tell myself, digging for the last ounce of courage deep inside.

Then the sun goes down and it grows blue-dark, then black-dark.

"On second thought, maybe I'll just die right here," I think.

Just then I see my husband jogging back toward me.

"You're doing great, Jan," he says, whizzing past. "You know, when I first started running, I could barely make it between telephone poles."

Suddenly I didn't feel so awful anymore. No wonder I'm still madly in love with that man. There are some dreams that should never die.

Chapter Five

School Days, School Daze, Dear Old Golden Rule Maze

Robert Fulghum became famous with an essay titled, "All I

Really Need To Know I Learned in Kindergarten." I've heard

it read at more school orientations, graduations, and church meetings than I care to remember. There's just one problem: Old Bob missed the mark. Fulghum failed to mention the greatest learning center of all. Yes, we do much of our important learning in those early years, and some of that learning takes place in kindergarten. But the greatest place to learn how to live and what to do and how to be will always be at home.

My kindergarten teachers didn't teach me to flush or to wash my hands before I ate, as Fulghum writes. My mother did that. My classmates didn't teach me to share; I learned that from my eight brothers and sisters. When I remember the Dick and Jane books, I don't recall that they taught me to "look." Even at five years old, I considered Dick and Jane books a limited-vocabulary curse for children. For I had listened to my father reading aloud the works of literary masters from his musty old Canadian readers as if the words were golden honey dropping from his tongue.

In school, I learned to color inside the lines according to the rules. I felt, breathed, and almost touched the vibrant colors of the sunset when my mother brought along a sketchbook and pastels as we hiked a southern Utah canyon trail at evening.

Now I am the parent with a house full of children, and I am relearning and teaching all the most important stuff right here in my own home. My children have given me the opportunity to reexperience the wonder of being new.

Through them, I am learning that it is never too late to have a happy childhood.

We should learn to clean up our own mess, according to Fulghum, and to put things back where we find them. Sound advice. But as a parent, I've learned that life is basically . . . messy. I can give up, or I can learn to make the best of things as they are. I've learned that people—especially children—rarely if ever put things back where they find them. I can despair over that, or rejoice in the eternal mystery of loss and gain.

Having school-age children introduces parents to a million challenges. One of those hazards is the dreaded science fair. Science teachers are basically well-intentioned adults. They truly believe that science-fair projects will arouse the dormant curiosity of our television generation and produce wonderful, brain-enlarged children, eager to discover the creations that will better mankind.

What really happens, though, is that about a zillion students are suddenly turned loose to grow mold in unsuspecting urban refrigerators, activate live volcanoes in darkened basements, and secretly perform undercover experiments on how many weeks one can wear the same pair of socks before they petrify. Science-fair season always begins with the annual note home to parents that stays crumpled in the bottom of the student's backpack. This note, which the student shows to the parents the night before the project is due, includes such important rules as these:

Rule 1. *Teachers, mentors, parents, etc., may advise but MUST NOT build or make any part of the exhibit.* Most parents are not troubled with this rule because most children are professional airheads who forget to tell parents they have a science-fair project due anyway. Children specialize in the seventeen-second "AHHHHHHHHHHHHHH! My science fair project is due today!" panic attack during breakfast while the school bus is honking in front of their house.

Rule 2. *Exhibits must be confined to a table or floor space not bigger than 36 inches wide by 30 inches deep. Maximum height is eight feet above the floor.* This rule doesn't affect me as a parent because the only thing my child has ever made higher than eight feet is a pile of dirty clothes, and this odoriferous mountain would certainly break Rule 3.

Rule 3. *Anything that could be hazardous to public display is prohibited.* I rest my case.

Rule 4. *Dangerous chemicals, open flames, explosives, and live, poisonous animals MUST NOT be exhibited.* Parents really appreciate this rule.

Rule 5. *Experiments on live animals must conform to the regulations for Experiments with Animals. Failure to do so will disqualify the exhibit.* Parents also love this rule, since children have been known to use the science-fair season as a convenient excuse for not feeding their pets.

Rule 6. *Plants must be watered.* This rule automatically disqualifies people like me who grow up to write books titled *Why Does My Mother's Day Potted Plant Always Die?* When I was a child, my first science-fair experiment was: "Why Do All My Father's Cherry Trees Die after I Chop Them Down with My Little Hatchet?"

Rule 7. *Exhibits will be evaluated on work done by students, not on value of accessory equipment. Criteria for judgment will be based on creative ability, scientific thought, thoroughness, skill, clarity, and visual appearance.* This rule truly endears science teachers to parents. Students who have to do their own work, have to do their own work. That leaves parents enough time to have their heads examined. Science-fair projects may create quite a stir on the home front, but where would our little "Albert Einstein in the making" be without them? Probably forced into beauty college until he learned how to comb his hair.

As long as we're in a list-making mood, let's look at another set of rules, the previously unwritten ones governing happy student-teacher relationships. Because most children will spend a great deal of their childhood as students, this is an important list for those who want to get on their teacher's good side.

Rule 1. *Abstain from dashing into class and yelling, "We're not going to do anything important today, are we?"*

This rule is especially true if you happen to be checking in on your way to a rip-roaring good time outside the classroom. Items on your person to avoid include motor-cycle helmets, tennis rackets, baseball gloves, and tickets to *Les Misérables*.

All teachers are arrogant enough to believe that their classes are significant and what they have to teach you is important. Actually, they figure if they had to show up for class, so should you. Teachers in this frame of mind often derive sinister pleasure from throwing a pop quiz just as you leave the room, tennis racket in hand, a foolish grin on your face. This spontaneous pop quiz will be worth roughly 95 percent of your final grade.

Rule 2. *Never preface any dialogue between you and your teacher with the following sentence: "I'm sorry I didn't get my assignment done, but I have a good reason."*

Teachers believe that the only legitimate excuse for not having completed an assignment is death. Because you are standing there talking, it is obvious to your teacher that you are not dead, and therefore your excuse is not good enough.

Rule 3. *Never ask the following question with a straight face: "Teacher, can I go to the bathroom?"*

Teachers have been known to offer all sorts of unpleasant responses to this seemingly innocent question, such as, "I hope so, young man." The correct way to phrase the question is, "Teacher, *may* I go to the bathroom?"

Teachers would prefer that you go before you leave home or enter the classroom, at recess, or on break. If you find yourself desperate in between, simply stand and walk toward the nearest rest room with as little fanfare as possible.

Rule 4. *Do not snore.*

When your teacher is in the midst of a mind-stimulating lecture, try to avoid drawing attention to yourself with strange noises escaping from your mouth or nose. Practice sleeping with your eyelids pried open with toothpicks. Even if your teacher is boring your socks off, by all means, leave your socks on.

Rule 5. *Learn the meaning of suffering and why it is necessary.*

Teachers know that you will experience more pleasure in life if you meet and experience pain first. Suffering is ultimately less painful than not suffering, so good teachers take it upon themselves to help students overcome gratification patterns formed in childhood.

Rule 6. *If you've had teachers who have had a positive effect on your life, let them know.*

I had a wonderful speech teacher at BYU who helped me learn that there is power in words, *even mine.* Years later I saw him singing with the Mormon Tabernacle Choir on television. I wanted to thank him, but he couldn't hear me. I took Drawing 101 from a graduate student who helped me discover the creator buried deep inside and the courage to express myself with honesty. I saw his obituary in the newspaper before I had a chance to tell him. I took

Statistics 552 from a master who led me through all those numbers and formulas with such graciousness and good humor that I came away triumphant, feeling I could tackle anything.

Those are some important rules for teacher-student relationships. Teacher-parent relationships, on the other hand, are a challenge that only creative parents can handle. Our children's school has a computer with a prerecorded message that calls students' homes and tells anyone who answers, "Hi, this is Spanish Fork High School calling to inform you that your student has been absent for one or more periods today."

I decided that if such a device is all right for the high school administrators, it's all right for us home administrators too. So I have a prerecorded message ready for use: "Hi, this is an automated parent responding to your call. If you want to hear a real parent, press 1. If you're calling to hear a fake parent, press 2."

Those who press 1 hear, "I realize that personality conflicts will occur occasionally during the school year. However, I must insist that teachers do not request that a student be assigned to another mother. Although some mothers might be happy with this arrangement, I've found that one mother is pretty much like another, and students and teachers will just have to learn to adjust."

Those who press 2 hear, "Any student dismissed to

come home sick from school will require a note from the school nurse verifying that the student is not faking it."

Here's another challenge of school days: School-age children quickly become professional holiday observers. Their parents, on the other hand, usually forget to wear green on St. Patrick's Day and would forget about Presidents' Day entirely if it weren't for the school-age set. Moms and dads tend to grow less enthusiastic as each holiday whizzes by. For instance, I'm a regular maternal Halloween dropout. My idea of a good time seldom includes sugar-crazed children roaming through my home. I've been watching those other, truly dedicated Halloween mothers and frankly, I just don't measure up. While they're busy recharging their video camera batteries to film the school costume parade, I'm still snoozing in bed trying to recharge my own batteries. While more noble parents are creating artistic displays with dried cornstalks, pumpkins, and scarecrows, I'm still trying to find the box marked *Halloween decorations*. I do this every year before I remember that I don't have a box marked *Halloween decorations* because I don't have any Halloween decorations. My children think they're deprived. They've been trying for years to get me into a class for Remedial Halloween Celebrators.

In all fairness, this lack of Halloween enthusiasm is not all my fault. For instance, one year my children picked all the pumpkins in our garden and threw them in the wheelbarrow right before it rained for two weeks. We ended up

with a wheelbarrow full of soggy orange rust bombs. The kids decided they'd make perfect objects for target practice.

Our cornstalks are still in the garden stalking. I'm afraid if I chop them down and make a front porch decoration, people will drive by and snicker. The first time I tried to be artistic on my front porch, strangers passing by hung their heads out of car windows, wrinkled their noses, and called, "What's that supposed to be?"

When my children saw the cornstalks and bales of hay, they figured I'd supplied them with new weapons for harpooning each other. Cornstalk and pumpkin wars can be ugly.

The closest I've come to making a scarecrow is my reflection in the front window when I'm waving good-bye to my elementary school kids in my ripped flannel nightgown. Talk about scary. I rent out for spook alleys, but don't get too excited. I'm all booked up for this year.

I've never been any good at creative suggestions for costumes, either. When my children ask, "Mom, what should I be for Halloween?" my answer is usually along the lines of, "Put a raisin in your belly button and go as a cookie."

My home is not totally devoid of creative scariness. The other night I opened the front door and found a skeleton rising from a yard or two of mud on my doorstep, holding a note that read, "I'd rise from the dead to go to Masquerade with you."

When I tried to walk into my daughter's bedroom, I ran

into a masking-tape barrier in her doorway that read, "Crime Scene, Do Not Enter!" There on the floor of her bedroom was the outline of a dead body on her rug with another note: "I'd kill to go to Masquerade with you."

This younger generation is a little more creative than their parents. When we asked someone to a high-school dance twenty years ago, our potential date just stood there with his face hanging out after we stopped him in the hall. "You wanna go to the dance with me?" "Uh, I guess so."

Maybe the world won't fall apart if we all do Halloween—or any other holiday for that matter—our way. My father used to tip over outhouses and rebuild them on top of the wrong owner's house. But the person I most admire is my sister-in-law, Melanie. One hot *July* afternoon when she was about three years old, she found herself completely out of candy. Melanie got dressed up, grabbed a brown bag, and went trick-or-treating. Her neighbors were a bit surprised but filled her bag all the same. Now, that's what I call a creative way to celebrate Halloween.

Children usually attend public schools for about thirteen years . . . thirteen years that someday will seem like roughly thirteen minutes. Each year, each holiday, each birthday seems to zip by a bit faster until we see our children, the greatest gifts God ever gave us, racing out the door to go on a mission, head for college, or get married. Suddenly we realize, sometimes too late, that we have had our children in our home for only a short time. We spend the rest of our lives wondering if we made the grade.

I know a mother of twelve who says she fears the judgment of her adult children more than the judgment of God. She says she often wonders if her grown children will say they became who they are *because of* or *in spite of* their parents.

I'll never forget the day my oldest daughter proudly announced that she was old enough to walk to school alone. "I can do it myself!" she insisted.

I didn't want to undermine her confidence by discouraging her, so I agreed. We walked together to the end of the block hand in hand, and then . . . she let go. I felt my heart sink to my toes. I knew we'd practiced hundreds of times looking both ways before crossing the street. I knew she was cautious and careful. I knew that holding her back when she felt ready would harm her more than help her. So, cheerfully waving, I called after her, "Wow! You're so grown-up. I love you."

My daughter turned, waved, and blew me a kiss. As she walked the several blocks to school, I followed close behind, dodging behind bushes so she wouldn't know I was following her. I watched her carefully following all our rules and safely navigating her way to the school grounds, across the grass, and in the front door.

When I turned and reluctantly dragged myself home that day, I couldn't stop the tears. Then a gentle realization

came to me. Maybe my heavenly parents were really peeking from behind the bushes to see if *I* made it home that day,
my heart aching. Even though I was unaware, maybe they
also were close, just out of sight, so I could let go . . . and do
it myself.

Chapter Six

Learning to Speak the Most Important Language

One of my big regrets for a long time was that I never

learned to speak a foreign language. Well, I may not know

Japanese, but I've come to realize that I have definitely been

studying an important language the past two decades, one

they don't teach at the university. I am fluent in the most difficult tongue of all: Childese. I often find myself translating
for other adults who don't understand this challenging language.

The other day at church, a frustrated teacher of small
tots was frantically trying to figure out what was wrong with
one of her crying students. The teacher looked at me in total
bewilderment, shook her head, and begged me to translate.

"He has to go to the bathroom," I answered. Nonverbal
communication speaks louder than words when you know
Childese.

"Is that it?" the teacher asked the tot. "Do you have to go
to the bathroom?"

The desperate child nodded. Teacher and child made a
mad dash for the little boy's room.

Even though I frequently translate for young children,
Childese also has higher-level skills.

"I hate you, Mom," my teen said the other day.

I knew that what she really meant was that she was
stuck in between childhood and adulthood, and that's hard
sometimes. What she really meant was that I'm one of the
few people she can spout off at and not worry that I'll quit
loving her. I know she loves me, and she knows I love her,
so I don't have to roll over and die when she expresses a dramatic, fleeting, negative feeling.

When you're fluent in Childese, you don't listen much
for actual words. You pay attention to the eyes. Once we had

an extra toddler running around the Baadsgaard house for a week while his parents went on vacation. He was just learning how to speak, and his mother spent most of the time before she left translating what he was saying.

It took me only a few minutes to learn this child's language. I didn't actually have to say anything, but when I found him alone in the hall with a long face, I made eye contact with him and smiled. He smiled back and gave me a hug. Sure, I spoke to him too. I told him what a fine fellow he was, and that I liked him, but the words didn't mean that much. It was the smile and the feeling behind the smile that made the connection.

You see, when you speak Childese you don't usually listen for the vocabulary, although that can prove helpful at times. People who speak this language can feel when someone is sad or lonely before they are told. They know when a teen just needs to spout off to someone. They know whether their little slugger won or lost the game without having to ask.

Those who speak Childese know when their baby's cry means hunger, fear, "I want my diaper changed," or "I'm tired and I've had it and I need to go to bed." They know that babies don't cry on purpose to annoy adults, and that if a baby keeps crying even after everything the adult can do, it doesn't mean the adult is an incompetent caregiver. Although I may never meet any formal graduation requirements,

I think my lifelong study of Childese is about the most important language training I will ever acquire.

Modern communication is serious business in families. Problem is, communicating with the outside world while on the homefront can sometimes be a bafflement. I answered the telephone the other day, for instance, and the person on the other end of the line grew strangely silent.

Right about the time I was about to hang up because I thought it was an obscene caller, the person sheepishly said, "Oh, I'm so sorry. I can't remember who I called. Could you tell me who you are?"

I guess I'd have been more annoyed if I hadn't done the same thing myself a dozen times. Telephones are supposed to be wonderful, life-simplifying inventions, but they more often complicate our lives. Take cordless phones, for example. Our family bought a new cordless telephone a few years ago, but after a few months we decided not to use it anymore. We were constantly having strangers break into our telephone conversations from other telephones. Then there was the problem of finding the darn thing after the kids had carried it off somewhere. We were always asking our neighbors to call us so we could hear the ringing and locate the cordless after some child had stuffed it under a couch cushion or a pile of dirty socks.

Several telephone-related maladies are quite common today. Take, for example, the *telepression* you feel when you dial directory assistance instead of trying diligently to find the number on your own. How about the *teleguilt* you feel when you hang up on a telephone solicitor? *Telelapse* is the period of complete silence between two people carrying on a telephone conversation while one person pretends to hunt for her day planner to write down an important message. (She's actually fumbling through her purse for an eyeliner and a tissue to write on.) This moment of silence also marks the time parents spend in mime techniques (grotesque facial expressions, hangman gestures with the phone cord) to intimidate their noisy children into quieting down.

Telecostitus strikes when you call someone long distance during normal business hours. This is the most expensive time of the day to call, so once you dial, you realize everything said is costing you prime-time money. *Teleguilt* kicks in and you end up saying things like, "Well, I'll be seeing you," and "Good-bye, my friend," at inappropriate times—like right after you've said "Hello."

Telesnore is the malady that strikes when you get on the line with a nonstop talker. *Telebow* develops when you've been holding a telephone receiver up to your ear for too long. *Telebow* is usually accompanied by *telear* and *teleneck*, or the weird paralysis that develops starting from your ear and running down your neck to your shoulder when someone calls and wants to tell you his or her life story.

Telefreeze is the condition that suddenly strikes a young child after she's been begging all week to phone Grandma and Grandpa and you finally put the receiver up to her ear.

She will suddenly become speechless and spitless, until you finally hang up in frustration, whereupon the child will break into tears because she didn't get to talk to Grandma or Grandpa.

What we really need is a national study on the long-term psychological maladies modern consumers develop as they contend with their trusted friend and loyal companion, the not-so-humble telephone.

Modern society has given us so much terrific technology. Problem is, some of this stuff is just one more way for children to drive their parents nuts. Take the telephone answering machine, for example. This innocent-looking convenience seems like such a good idea . . . until you actually buy one.

"Wouldn't it be great to know who's calling when I'm stuck in the bathroom?" I told my husband a few months before we bought the cordless. "I can't tell you how many times I've dashed out of the bathroom just in time to have the caller hang up on me."

"I'd like to screen those obnoxious telephone solicitors," my husband answered. "It really bugs me the way those guys always call during the dinner hour to sell electric lightbulbs, carpet cleaning, or family portraits."

"Due to the fact that my phone calls are the only truly important modern communication made to this family," my teenage daughter interrupted, "I'd like to make sure I don't miss any more calls from my friends, especially the good-looking, male kind."

"Hey, yeah," my elementary-school-age son added. "That way I won't have to take down any more messages for April."

Dummies that we are, we actually bought a telephone answering machine. My life has never been the same since.

The first little problem came to light when I politely answered the telephone the other day. The caller on the other end said, "Oh, darn. Why did you have to answer? I just called to hear your answering machine message. Word's around that it's a pretty good one."

I was a little suspicious after that call, so I listened to the recorded message on our machine. I found out the kids had recorded themselves screaming bloody murder while one sibling yelled into the machine, "Help! You've reached the Baadsgaard residence. We're all being held hostage! If we don't return your message, call 911!"

When I told my son to record something a little more dignified and polite on the machine, he smiled and said, "Sure thing, Mom."

This son never says, "Sure thing, Mom," so I decided I'd better check up on him. Sure enough, he had obeyed his mother and recorded a new message on the machine. This time the message said, "This is the Baadsgaard Fruit of the Loom Factory. So please be brief."

After a few stern lectures, I thought I'd finally gotten through to the children and convinced them that we shouldn't insult our callers by being so silly. Things were going pretty well until I noticed the blinking red light on the answering machine the other day, signifying that we had received an actual message from a caller. Our previous messages had been a long series of phone-hanging-up clicks. No one actually called to talk to us; they just wanted to hear our latest recorded message.

I pushed the button and waited to hear the first intelligent message left by our first intelligent caller. What I heard was a series of hog-snout grunts. I hung up in a huff and instantly flagged down my "Fruit of the Loom" son.

"I don't know how you did it," I said, sternly wagging my finger in his face, "but I don't want you leaving hog-snout grunts on the telephone answering machine anymore. Do you understand me, young man?" Of course, "Brief" didn't own up to any of this nonsense.

When I told my husband about it later that night, his neck turned red and he reluctantly owned up to the little hog-mating-call caper. No wonder I can't get through to these children of mine. It's in their genes.

Kids have it pretty darn tough today. Sometimes we parents forget just how hard it is to grow up. We fail to communicate to our children that we understand them because down deep we're still children too. Just when our kids start having a little fun, we parents jump in with such spoilsport comments as, "If you don't turn off that electric drill and quit chasing your brother, you're going to be in big trouble, young man."

Just when our kids start enjoying their supper, we excessively serious parents ruin all the fun with totally unsolicited comments like, "Get that glass of red punch off your head—now!"

Childhood and adolescence would run a little smoother if children would just understand this one fact: Parents don't really care if our children are murdering each other, as long as they die quietly and clean up after themselves.

Parents tend to get agitated with all the chaos and clutter that family life brings and have been known to fly off the handle and say such cruel things as, "I don't care if it's not fair." We long-suffering parents do not want you children to leave our home until you have the complete, detailed understanding that when we were young, we had to get off the couch and walk all the way over to the television set to change the channel.

Children need to exercise a little patience and consider that parents don't remember what it's like to have a major zit breakout on picture day at school. We can't remember the last time we worried about being asked to the prom or forgetting our locker combination.

There are certain advantages of adult life that parents are afraid to mention. For instance, not once in the past twenty-five years has anyone forced me to pass off a cartwheel for valuable P.E. points when I have trouble walking and chewing gum at the same time. I don't have to shower in front of all the other girls my age in town. I never worry about making the team. I can frequent nonschool rest rooms, free of the worry that toilet-paper bombs stuck on the ceiling will drop on my head, or that someone is peeking over or under my stall door.

In truth, we adults just forget how tough it is to survive growing up because we're bogged down in adultness. We're all wrapped up in comparing toothpaste prices, paying the telephone bill, staying up late with sick children, and keeping gas in the car. We walk around like robots doing the dishes and taking out the garbage without being threatened with bodily harm. Sometimes it gets kind of boring. We cook supper, sort darks from the lights, hold down jobs, act responsible, remember who we are, sit up straight, fly right, and have respect for ourselves. It's not easy, but somebody has to do it.

Funny thing, though: Occasionally we adults have a recurring nightmare. We dream we're walking down the hall at school in our underwear. Or we dream that we can't remember our locker combination, or that we're trying to take a final exam for a class we have forgotten to attend all semester.

Maybe, deep down inside, we remember that it's tough growing up after all.

Chapter Seven

Opening Doors

If you take the time to notice the doors in your home, you

can learn more about your family than if you spent hours

reading Dr. Spock. For example, if your child has a qua-

druple heart attack when you try to close the door at bed-

time, you know you are dealing with a highly imaginative,

easily frightened toddler or preschooler. If your child myste-

riously closes and locks his own door at bedtime and you

turn into a highly imaginative, easily frightened parent, you know you have a teenager in the house.

If someone tapes written messages to the bedroom door that read "Enter and Die!" or "Stay Out and That Means You!" or "This Is My Room, You Hairy Good For Nothing Sneak, So Keep out!" you know your husband is going through a midlife crisis.

Bathroom doors are a great gauge to inform parents about their children's latest and strangest physical development. If your bathroom door is never locked and your child invites you inside to witness and applaud, you know you have toddlers and preschoolers in the house. If you haven't seen the inside of the hall bathroom for years because someone is always in there with the water running and the door locked, you know you have teens lurking about on your premises.

Refrigerator doors are a less helpful means of decoding your children's developmental levels, because once your children learn to open the refrigerator door—at approximately six weeks of age—you'll swear the Mona Lisa is in there smiling next to the milk jugs, based on the amount of time your children stand and stare.

Car doors, however, are an excellent measure of your child's stage of development. If your car door stays closed while you're driving somewhere, you have an infant in the family. If you have mass murders in the backseat over who gets to sit by the door, you have children aged twelve months to nineteen years. If you can't open the car door from the outside because someone has been messing with the lock mechanism again and lost the little up-and-down-knob, you have children.

Returning to the house, if you have holes in the Sheetrock directly behind every door in your home, you have children.

If you yell, "Close that door!" about one zillion times a day, you have children.

If you yell, "Open that door!" because it's too quiet and they must be up to something, you have children.

If you have doorknobs that won't work because somebody has been cramming bobby pins, pencils, spaghetti ends, and crayons into the lock, tell your husband to splurge and buy a screwdriver.

When I was a harried mother of six children, all under eight years of age, I once ushered all my noisy kids outside into the fenced play area and told them to stay out there until I collected my wits. Then I closed and locked the sliding glass door and sat where I could keep my eye on them. All six children solemnly sat down on the steps next to the glass door and hung their heads. Then, at the same instant, they all turned around and smashed their little greasy noses and lips on the glass. It reminded me of the algae-eating fish my mother had bought for our aquarium. I couldn't help myself. I unlocked the door and let them back inside.

"Got your wits yet?" one of the children asked.

Doors are a great way to find your wits and open your eyes when you're a parent. What you find when you open that parental door is always worth knocking for.

Another door my children have opened for me is realizing that winning is not everything. We've all heard it a hundred times, "Winning isn't everything: it's the only thing." We see the effects of this lame logic in political campaigns, business dealings, world politics, family relationships, and sports.

Fame, money, and power have become an obsession. The constant drive to win or get ahead, whatever the cost, is destroying our ability to honor or even notice what really matters.

A number of my children have played in a variety of school, community, and church sponsored basketball games. Sitting in the stands watching these games and listening to myself and other parents has taught me a lot more than the score at the end of the game.

During one of our children's basketball games, a father of a child on the opposing team turned to my husband and said, "Your kid has a nice soft shot. But you should take him out in the backyard and play a little one-on-one with him. Teach him to play a little more aggressively, you know what I mean—go for the jugular."

I sat and listened to this same man bad-mouth the referees play after play. His child was later thrown out of the game when he intentionally shoved another player into a brick wall. He'd been taught well.

Our local news broadcasts mirror our warped priorities. We give the majority of our news time to reports about the bad things people do to each other, spotlighting criminals and perverts, breaking long enough to list the scores and relive the highlights of endless sporting events. We shell out our time, money, and admiration to actors, musicians, and sports heroes who cater to our lowest instincts.

Where are our statesmen, our honest businessmen, and our dedicated parents? Where are our great thinkers, writers, teachers, and inventors? They're still around, but we don't notice or honor them anymore. Our world spins on a dime. We've forgotten compassion, kindness, patience, and tolerance.

There is nothing more influential in a child's life than the power of quiet example. If our children are going to take morality seriously, they must be in the presence of parents who take morality seriously. We give our money, time, and adoration to things we love. When we love self-discipline, courage, honesty, hard work, faith, and compassion more than we love popular opinion, fame, prestige, leisure, wealth, and power, we will create a new generation that mirrors our beliefs.

That's why it meant so much to me when a wise parent from the sidelines stopped my son after a recent basketball game and said, "I want to congratulate you on the way you played that game, young man. You were a real gentleman."

Three of our babies died before they were born. Their passing opened a door of understanding for me. I am now acutely aware of the miracle of life and how quickly it can be taken. I remember that lesson some days better than others, and when I do, the door of appreciation opens and I see my life and my children with new eyes.

When I see through the eyes of gratitude, I take the time to hold chubby cheeks in the palms of my hands. When I look out my bedroom window and view the dormant winter fields around my home, I notice the quiet beauty that precedes spring. All the muted shades in that quiet space between seasons hold a gentle peace, easily missed. The dried, golden grass and gray, weathered fence posts form a still and tranquil landscape.

I want to notice the beauty of every season of my life, from the first daffodil or forsythia blossom to the last weathered leaf in the wind. I don't want to miss the look on my two-year-old's face as she cradles the softness of a new bunny against her skin. I don't want to ignore the strength and dignity of my aging parents as they face the effects of palsy and Parkinson's disease with quiet courage and faith.

When I wake up to all the everyday miracles around me, all the mundane household chores I usually perform on "automatic pilot" take on new meaning. Doing the laundry keeps me intimately in touch with my children's triumphs and tragedies, from skinned knees to burgeoning adolescence. Wiping the kitchen floor for the third time in one day keeps me on my knees, where I get my most private answers.

The only time I have is now. I may have to leave all this at any moment. None of us know how long we will be able to stay. I can't wait for tomorrow to embrace the day.

A young mother in my area recently had serious complications following the birth of her fifth child, and began slipping away in the hospital in spite of everything the doctors could do. "I can't die now!" this young mother pleaded to her husband. "I have to go home and tell the kids I'm sorry and I love them."

This young mother worried that she'd been too harsh on her family in the days before she went into labor. She wanted one last chance to go home and express her love. She got that privilege, but she died suddenly two months later.

Life is a fragile gift. Like the seasons that pass over the fields around my home, there is meaning and beauty in all phases of life. The simple things, like friends and family, are what give life meaning. Knowing that we will all have to leave someday should instill in us the urgency of giving our undivided attention as we welcome, with gladness, each new day.

My daughter Amy has opened a family door to the tenderness of good-byes. Amy has a ritual she performs every time someone leaves our house for any reason. It doesn't matter if you're walking outside to get the mail or if you'll be gone for several days. If you put on a coat, grab your purse, or stand up and walk toward the door, Amy will immediately run to your side in sheer panic and plead, "I need a kiss and hug!"

Amy's request must not be taken lightly. She simply cannot bear to see any of us leave the house without an intimate show of genuine physical affection. Mind you, not just any sort of hug and kiss will do. The hug must be of the wrap-your-arms-around-the-neck variety, and the kiss must be one to knock your socks off. You can't fake it, because Amy will keep calling you back until you get it right.

Once, when I was in a hurry, I tried to sneak out of the house before Amy noticed. But Amy has extrasensory perception. When I was halfway out the door, she appeared out of nowhere, grabbed my leg, and held on for dear life.

"Just kiss my leg," I said, trying to shake her off. "I'm in a hurry, Amy. I'm going to be late." Amy would not let go until I did it right.

After all this hugging and kissing stuff, Amy will move into the next phase of her ritual, which involves racing to the front-room window, parting the curtains, and waving. If you don't wave back, Amy will cry, hard, for at least a solid hour.

Amy has trained her family well. No one slams the front door without hugging and kissing or races out of our driveway without looking up at the front-room window, waving and throwing kisses.

Amy's little sister Ashley has been taking night classes from her older role model. Now, instead of one voice screaming, "I need a kiss and hug!" we have a vocal duet. It takes twice as long to get out the door.

All this good-bye stuff and waving business used to bug the tarnation out of the whole family. We were always saying things like, "Amy, I can't. I'm in a hurry. I'll hug you when I get home. For heaven's sake, Amy, relax. I'll be right back. Oh, Amy."

But Amy won out in the end. Because of her persistence and insistence, the whole family has readjusted routines and priorities. We all give ourselves a few extra minutes before we leave now, because we know parting is such sweet sorrow at our house.

All this attention by our twosome has a way of making the rest of the family feel rather downright loved. And once you get used to it, hugging and kissing isn't so bad after all. In fact, these days, if Amy and Ashley happen to be busy playing with their dolls and don't notice one of us leaving, we'll search through the house for those two sets of soft, chubby arms before we feel like facing the cold, cruel world out there.

"Where are Amy and Ashley?" I hear my older children, my husband, and myself say when we leave the house. What we mean is: "I need a kiss and hug."

We all need to be acknowledged and cared for. Though we quit asking for it as we grow older, we all need lots of love and someone standing in the front-room window blowing kisses when we close the door and walk away.

Chapter Eight

Comrades in Arms

Parents and soldiers have a lot in common. When you first

become a parent, you mistakenly assume you'll eventually

move up in the ranks and someday be given command.

Your delusions of holding a high-ranking position quickly

evaporate in the face of hard reality. You learn that you are

at best a lowly enlisted man. In time, all parents realize that

no one is saluting, and that even two-year-olds laugh

when their parents bark out orders. Respect comes about thirty years later, if at all.

Combat rations are slim pickings for parents after the troops vacuum up every morsel in sight. Parents can't even complain about the lousy food because they worked for it, cooked it, and cleaned up the mess afterward. Latrine duty is even tougher for parents in arms than for soldiers; at least all the army guys are potty trained.

Parents, like soldiers, are forced to pick up the remains of atomic blasts (slumber parties) and spend long hours in confined quarters undergoing exquisite torture (the family vacation). Parents must also learn secret codes to unravel the other side's communication systems and develop the ability to understand all ages and levels of intelligence at a moment's notice.

Parents are rarely given any weapons except perhaps a raised spatula to ward off sibling water-balloon and popcorn air raids. Down in the rough and dirty trenches of family life, parents have been known to suffer all kinds of deprivation, including sleep loss and surprise stomach-flu attacks. If you don't think parents everywhere have to find their way through mine fields, try walking across a living-room floor after a four-year-old has booby-trapped the carpet with six million Legos.

Dedicated parents, unlike soldiers, are never awarded purple hearts or medals for valor. Their rewards are wet kisses, dirty socks, and used tissues. Parents don't get ticker-tape parades or granite monuments. They never even know before they die if they won or lost the battle; families go on forever, and there's always a chance that Junior will change his wild ways before he kicks the bucket. There are no decorated veterans of family life because parents simply move onward and upward to the ranks of grand and great.

Not only are moms and dads soldiers in the trenches together, I have it on expert authority that they also make the best lovers. For those of us married folks who house, clothe, and feed several children, the challenge to keep the fire burning takes a little more kindling, but romance doesn't have to go up in smoke.

There are warning signs to watch for: When your weekly dates have degenerated to grocery-shopping trips at Barney's Bargain Barn, and your passionate kisses have melted into notes stuck to the refrigerator door, it's time for a romantic interlude. When you can't remember the last time you and your spouse spent a romantic evening together without someone yelling, "Mom, come button me up!" or "Dad, I just didn't see that other car before it was too late!" you know it's time to fly the coop.

"I've got us a room," my husband whispered while I was down on my hands and knees wiping the kitchen floor a while back. "Go pack." Those have to be some of the sweetest words a spouse can utter.

After we packed, loaded the car, said good-bye to the children, and headed north on the freeway, I turned to Ross and said, "I feel like I've forgotten something . . . like about 900 pounds of kids."

Ross turned to me and winked. "I've got you and you've got me. What else could we possibly need?"

I shivered like a new bride.

When we marry and have families, we soon become blessed and burdened with all kinds of responsibilities and pressures. Too quickly we lose sight of what brought us together in the first place. I glanced over at Ross in the driver's seat and saw him again for the first time. There sat my husband, the father of my children, my lover, my dearest friend, and the kindest, most interesting man I know.

Then Ross reached over and took my hand. The warmth of that gentle, masculine hand took me back through the years. I remembered the day those hands held mine across the wedding altar. I remembered the day he adjusted his graduation cap and gown while he balanced his two baby daughters on his lap. I remembered his high-five the day I sold my first book. I remembered those hands letting go of our son on his first solo flight on a two-wheeler. I remembered those hands cradling our new babies as he rocked them to sleep. Those hands have led me up every mountain in Utah and through the valley of childbirth. And when three of our children didn't survive birth, those hands gently cradled my head on his shoulder and tenderly comforted me. I cherish my husband's hands.

Later, we enjoyed a restaurant meal—which someone

else cooked, served, and cleaned up after—followed by the miracle of a whole uninterrupted day and night to shop, talk, and hold each other.

Raising a family makes private romantic time more eloquent and dear. As the years go by, it's easy to begin thinking of our spouse's purpose only as it exists in relation to ourselves: "My wife should take care of me." "My husband should bring home a salary." "My wife should keep the house clean and the kids fed." "My husband should make me happy." The list goes on and on. It has taken me many years to understand this, but I now realize that Ross has a reality and destiny basically separate from my own. He has potential that he needs to fulfill both within *and* apart from our union. His purpose is to grow, stretch, and become all he can be, not just for my benefit but to the glory of God. And the same is true for me. Mature relationships between husbands and wives are like two people making music together: the harmony can be beautiful, but each has his or her own instrument to play.

Years ago, I found Ross sitting at the side of our bed, his head in his hands. My father-in-law had been in critical care at the hospital for weeks. Running back and forth to the hospital, not knowing what he would find, had taken a heavy toll on my husband.

"Are you all right?" I asked.

"Oh, it's nothing. Just stupid, really," Ross answered. "I was walking back to the house from the barn when I saw

Dad's old *Baadsgaard Realty* sign leaning against the house. I realized Dad wasn't going to be around much longer."

I sat down next to him and moved over until our shoulders touched. We sat together in silence, like two trees facing the wind. I realized that, though we were both ultimately alone in our pain, we could share our vulnerability in private ways known only to those who share the same dreams, the same children, and the same bed. Two pillars, side by side— or a husband and wife sitting together at the edge of the bed—can bear a burden that would be too heavy for one.

I remembered an evening when Ross and I went for a walk together on the country roads that surround our house. The western sky was beginning to turn amber and wheat-colored as the sun set. Ross likes to run. I prefer walking. Near the end of our walk, I looked up into my husband's eyes and knew he'd been walking instead of running to please me, to give us time to be together. I also knew he wanted to run.

"Go ahead, Ross," I insisted. "I'll catch up to you around the bend."

So Ross broke ahead, jogging up the hill ahead of me. Moments later I looked up and saw him just at the crest of the hill, a black silhouette against the wide, red sky. He was alone, beautiful, free. I knew that we were on the same road together, that we would meet up soon before we reached home. But we each had our own way, our own speed.

I felt overcome with a depth of love for my husband that

is hard to describe in words. I felt his oneness with me, his tender hopes, fears, and dreams; his goodness, vulnerability, and strength. I found in myself no disposition to dominate or resent his agency. I knew that our companionship gave us eternal opportunities to be servants to each other, to influence the formation of each other's souls most deeply. I felt a desire to be a refuge for him, to be friends without end in the bonds of love.

Just then Ross turned and held his arms out to me. I had to give it a shot. I mustered up all my courage and ran toward him. No Hollywood music made a crescendo; the stillness of the country air was interrupted only by the sound of my out-of-shape huffing and puffing. But slowly I made it to the crest of the hill and fell into the shelter of his embrace.

"Look," Ross whispered, pointing to the golden red glow in the western horizon.

There we stood, arms around each other, gazing into the sunset until Olsens' sheep truck honked us off the road. For a moment I think we both understood what it meant to truly *feel* life—to throw ourselves into the mystery and glimpse where it might take us. Though we understood that life has no guarantees, and that things don't always work out, we also knew of warmth, light, laughter, and joy in the sanctuary of each other's love.

Chapter Nine

On the Tilt-a-Whirl with Teens

When Rudyard Kipling wrote, "If you can keep your head

when all about you are losing theirs and blaming it on you,"

I think he had parents of teenagers in mind. Teenagers are

very confusing people stuck somewhere between childhood

and adulthood, so parents tend to get bewildered a lot.

One day you glance around and notice you're the shortest person in the kitchen. You have to take a number to get into the bathroom. Every time you try to kiss your child, his lips are higher. Every time you go to the refrigerator, empty shelves stare back at you. Your head pounds to the beat of the stereo, and nobody asks you for your advice or a Snoopy Band-Aid to make it all better.

"Just wait till you have teenagers. You ain't seen nothing yet," I heard over and over until I wanted to run up the white flag *before* my first daughter even turned thirteen. I wasn't ready to listen to these harder-times-ahead stories when I was trying to survive newborns, toddlers, and elementary-school-age children. I used to think, How could a child who can use the bathroom unassisted be all bad? How could a child who doesn't require hand feeding every two hours be someone to complain about?

Time passed, and something happened. My daughter walked in the door, and I greeted her with my usual, "Well, how was school today, dear?"

She scowled at me and replied, "Why do you want to know?"

A week or two later I asked her if she wanted to go shopping with me.

She looked me over from head to toe and replied, "Not if you're going to go dressed like that."

I was beginning to get suspicious. In the past, I had had to drag her into the bathroom for baths. Suddenly she began staying in the bathroom so long her younger brothers and sisters mistook her for one of the fixtures and tried to throw their dirty clothes on her. She locked herself in her bedroom for hours to talk on the telephone.

When I asked her to help me with the dishes, she shouted back, "I hate this family! You don't understand me. Why don't you just get off my back?"

Even though I now have a house full of teens, I find myself inflicted with terminal flashback-itis. Every time my daughter struts proudly around the house in the latest hairstyle and fashion statement, I can't help but remember how she looked in four layers of diapers as she waddled down the hall toward her crib.

When she screams, "Get off my back," I can't help remembering when she used to gently pat my cheeks, rub her pug nose against mine, and say, "I love you, Mommy, bigger than a brontosaurus."

When she gets embarrassed to show me to her friends because I wear geeky polyester pants and orthopedic shoes, I remember the time she danced around our yard in the front of the neighbors without wearing anything at all.

Being the parent of teens is sometimes the loneliest occupation on earth. You may be sitting there with half a dozen happy, crazy adolescents throwing paper airplanes, popcorn, and darts, eating pizza and green olives . . . but as soon as you suggest, "Hey, let's clean up," everyone dissolves into thin air.

It wasn't always like this. When my children were young, they were always following me around begging to be allowed to vacuum, dust, and clean. But when they were old enough to be of any real help, the offers stopped and never came again.

Now that my children are old enough to clean things properly, they don't see any point to it. Whenever I say, "Why don't you make your bed before you leave?" they answer, "But Mom, I'm just going to crawl back into it and mess it all up again in a few hours anyway."

When I finally get them to make their beds, I ask, "Why do you make your bed up and over your clean clothes?"

They say, "Well, Mom, you're the one who keeps putting all those clean clothes on the foot of my bed. What else do you expect me to do?"

They say, "You always want everything so perfect, Mom. Well, I like a little mess. What's more, I like a lot of mess."

I say, "All I want is a clear path through the clutter so I won't trip and fall when I get up in the night with the baby."

"Well, it's your fault," they chide me. "You're the one who always wanted a big family."

When my children finally reach the age when I've trained them to be built-in baby-sitters, they find better-paying jobs elsewhere. When I want to go somewhere, any-where, without half a dozen small children Velcroed to my arms and legs, my teenage children have a waiting list of paying customers. I make them work without paying them a measly dime.

My adolescent children also remind me of the Blob. The Blob is a large glob of near-motionless matter used in the old movies to scare unsuspecting adults. It always sneaks up when they have their backs turned.

When I ask, "Have you . . . (done your homework, made your bed, practiced the piano)?" there is no response. The child sits in the chair and becomes the Blob, an expressionless, emotionless glob. I'm afraid to kick it to see if it's still alive, for fear it will ooze over to me and suck me into oblivion.

But there are other times—times when I hear the piano actually being played without promise of reward or punishment, times when someone says, "What can I do to help you, Mom?" Every once in a while I see a wet towel hung up or a smelly sock that made it to the hamper without my assistance. After I check a few foreheads for fever, I'm in love again.

One of the hardest rites of passage for parents of adolescents is allowing their teens to actually drive the family car. No child ever seems old enough or mature enough.

When my sixteen-year-old daughter and I presented her application for a driver's license the other day at the Motor Vehicle Division, no one intimidated her or forced her into a strange car with an unknown man for a road test. No one tested her at all. They'd taken care of all that at her high school beforehand. All she had to do was take an eye exam, pay her fee, and have her photo taken.

I felt like shaking every adult in the government building and yelling, "For heaven's sake, people, why are you willing to give this child a license? She hasn't got a clue. Can't you change the laws or something, change the age restrictions?"

The other day this same sixteen-year-old daughter told me that a teacher at school had told her class to go home and look at their parents. "That's the way you're going to look in twenty years," the teacher said, "so be kind."

My daughter said all the students in the class yelled things like, "Oh, no! Please, don't tell me that! What is there to live for?"

"I pictured you and Dad," my daughter said, "and I thought, *well, they're not too bad.*"

I remember the evening when my husband and I were taking our junior-high-age daughter to her spring choral concert. About a block before we got to the school she shouted, "Stop! Let me out here. You guys can park and come in later. And don't sit on the front row and wave and take pictures."

As our daughter raced to the school doors, we looked at each other in shock. Our daughter didn't want to be seen walking into the school with us. She was afraid we would do something to embarrass her in front of the whole community. Where had we gone wrong? Had we really become geeks?

We suddenly realized that our daughter was ashamed of having parents. Once we quit being ashamed of having a daughter who was ashamed of having parents, a whole new world opened. Recognizing our new position of power in her life, we parked and walked into the school—after pulling our pants up to our armpits and positioning our jaws to look like we had horrible overbites. Then we found a place to sit on the front row.

"Hi, honey!" I yelled before the concert began. "Hey, everybody, that's my daughter. Yoo-hoo! Smile!"

Ross flashed the camera and went in for a close-up.

Being the parents of teenagers is a lot more fun when you quit feeling bad about having become a geek and sort of revel in it. Parents of adolescents see their offspring through braces, glasses, driver's training, slumber parties, grades, ACT tests, college rejections, proms, car accidents, late nights, birds-and-the-bees chats, marathon phone calls, speeding tickets, boyfriends/girlfriends or the lack of the same, strange fashion statements and hairstyles, and the constant need for cash. Teens should reciprocate by patiently enduring their parents' embarrassing geekiness.

Living with teens can leave you feeling like you just stepped off a Tilt-a-Whirl, but it's worth the dizziness because, frankly, it's the only known way to get an adult child.

Over and over again we parents of teens need to tell ourselves: Be patient. Our frustration, fear, worry, pain, disappointment, and panic will soon turn into frustration, fear, worry, pain, disappointment, and panic about entirely new issues. And if we hang in there, someday soon grandchildren will be our reward for not killing our teenagers.

Chapter Ten

Endings and Beginnings

December always brings closure to another year but the

opening of most parental states of overwhelm. If, after all the

hustle and bustle of shopping, baking, sitting through long,

stuffy programs, and attending an endless series of parties,

you feel like you want to stop the holiday wagon and jump—

if you're paying attention, something will happen to make it all worthwhile. One December evening when I finally finished my nightly wiping up of slop, heave-ho, and potato cement from under the dinner table, I slipped into the living room alone. All the children were scattered around the house, some yelling, some hibernating, and others imitating sumo wrestlers. I pushed the hair away from my face with my dishpan hands and took a slow, deep breath before I sat down and began quietly playing Christmas hymns on the piano. The music must have slipped through the heat vents, for one by one the children spontaneously wandered into the living room. Except for a single brass light above the piano, the living room was dark. The hard wooden piano bench soon grew warm and crowded as my two-year-old snuggled up on my right side while her ten-year-old sister squeezed in on my left. Then the baby crawled across the carpet, elbowed her way through my legs, and started playing with my big toe as it bobbed up and down on the sustaining pedal. Seven- and eight-year-old sumo wrestlers untangled themselves and tumbled into the room long enough to belt out a few tunes standing guard behind me.

You've never really heard "Joy to the World" until you've heard a seven-year-old, with total abandon and a little off key, command from the depths of his soul, *"Joy to the world! The Lord is come! Let earth receive her king! Let every heart repair him room! And saints and angels swing!"* Later, when our voices were tired and squeaky, we did "Silent Night," complete with "Round John Virgin." As we rounded the corner to *"Sleep in heavenly peace; Sleep in heavenly peace,"* it hit: that skin-tingling, hold-your-breath moment when the magic, mystery, and wonder of Christmas was mine.

At that precise moment, it didn't matter that our budget was having a hard time stretching for a family of eleven. It didn't matter that within seconds my "heavenly choir" would return to sumo wrestling on the living-room floor. For I had learned that moments like these are fleeting. Like winter's frost, with a breath, childhood melts away. So I sighed, detached the baby from my toe, and kissed all those Junior Tabernacle Choir members on the forehead before they could pull away yelling, "Yuck, kissing. I hate kissing." Christmas comes but once a year. With or without the mistletoe, you have to grab those kisses while you can.

Soon, without warning, Christmas is over. Christmas decorations, mental health experts report, often produce a seasonal character disorder in parents. Psychiatrists report a dramatic increase in their workloads during January. Patients come to them with a sense of helplessness, unable to cope with such post-holiday hassles as dry pine needles, fake snow, burnt candles, and one more cinnamon gummy Santa stuck to the sofa.

Otherwise sane adults are suddenly unable to schedule the pain of life in such a way as to enhance their pleasure. In other words, nobody wants to put the Christmas stuff away. Delaying the painful process of boxing up Christmas is universal. Even saintly mothers find themselves scream-ing, "If I took all my Christmas decorations out of these boxes six weeks ago, why don't they fit when I try to put them back?"

I used to routinely put all my Christmas decorations up the day after Thanksgiving and take them down on the sec-ond day of January. These days I find myself picking up the miniature village on the fireplace mantle and mumbling, "I like these houses here. I believe I'll just keep them up for another eleven years or so."

Parents also face the overwhelming responsibility of deciding which Christmas masterpieces to throw out and which to save. Moms and dads are positively sure that if they trash Junior's 167th paper snowflake or toilet-paper-roll Santa, the child will grow up and sue them for unloving behavior unbecoming a parent.

Now I understand why my parents never took down the outside Christmas lights when I was growing up. By the time I came along, they'd discovered creative uses for the lights year round. They found if they flashed the multi-colored lights draped around the rain gutters in July, their daughter lingering outside in the car with her date would suddenly race to the door without so much as a single parental threat.

Each year I decide to leave one more elf, sleigh bell, or gingerbread house up all year. Who says you can't have a Halloween tree or a miniature lighted village complete with electric train running through Easter Egg Subdivision, American Flag Flats, or Turkey Condo Heaven? To live joyously—or at least to avoid the pain of finding enough storage space for all your holiday stuff—you must find creative ways to use Christmas decorations all year long.

Last July I discovered ancient Christmas lights left in our front yard pine tree by the previous owners of our house. The tree had since grown several feet outward, hiding the lights. I don't know why, but I started singing "Silent Night" after I finished weeding around the base. Then I reached into the tree, fingered one of those old lights in my dirt-covered hand, and whispered, "Thanks, I needed that." We all need a little Christmas . . . all year long.

My most memorable Christmas was the one I now affectionately call the stomach-flu Christmas. Six weeks before that cold Christmas eve, I had given birth to my son Jacob. This pregnancy had been particularly long and difficult because my doctor had ordered bed rest to prevent Jacob's premature delivery. After seven pregnancies in eight years, this Christmas season found me exhausted and discouraged. It seemed I didn't have the time, health, or money to do the things I thought were truly important for the kind of Christmas I wanted for my children.

I dreamed about the picture-perfect Christmas I'd seen in Hollywood movies or read about in books. But a postpartum bleeding problem, a lingering infection, and a house full of overactive young children left me feeling chronically overwhelmed. After paying off the doctors and hospital, we didn't have much money left over for gifts. I'd been sewing dolls from cloth scraps and painting blocks and toy trucks from leftover wood ends in the wee hours between late-night feedings and fussy sessions with my newborn son.

Then, on Christmas Eve, it hit like a blast of Arctic air: the dreaded stomach flu. All my children suddenly became violently ill. They were too young or too weak to reach the bathroom, so I rushed from bed to crib diapering, changing sheets, and comforting the best I could.

Then the illness hit me just as hard. I soon found myself unable to stand without fainting. I must have hit my head on the corner of our nightstand passing out, because my forehead was throbbing and had a lump forming when I woke up on the floor in my bedroom.

For a moment I lay motionless on the floor, paralyzed with nausea, cramping, and throbbing pain. Then I tried to figure out what I should do. If I called someone for help, I would expose friends or family to the dangerous condition of the ice-covered roads and this awful illness. My husband had been out of town on a business trip and should have been home hours ago. Because he hadn't called, I worried he might be stranded on the road somewhere or in an accident.

I felt overwhelmingly sick, alone, and afraid. "Mom! Mom! Help me!" I heard my children crying in their rooms.

"Dear Father in Heaven," I prayed. "Why does everything have to be so hard, especially on Christmas Eve?"

"Mommy! I need you!"

"Please give me the strength," I prayed. "My children need me." I raised my head and felt another fainting spell coming on, so I maneuvered my body into a kneeling position. If I kept my head down, I could slowly crawl from bed to bed. Hours passed with no break. Around midnight, I heard the front door open and my husband trudge toward the back of the house. I was lying in a near fetal position on the floor in the hallway next to the children's bedrooms so that I could hear and respond to their needs. My newborn son, Jacob, was wrapped in a blanket and cradled in the bend of my body. My husband rushed into the bathroom, collapsed on the bed, and moaned. He wouldn't be able to help. He was as sick as the rest of us.

Just then I heard the pendulum clock in the family room begin the first of twelve soft chimes. When the clock grew silent, I knew Christmas had come. I didn't have the strength to put gifts under the tree, and the stockings were still empty, but my children were sleeping peacefully for the first time that evening. I felt the slow breaths from my infant son blowing gently on my neck. Clouds parted in the night sky outside just enough to let a faint bit of moonlight filter into the hallway. "It's Christmas," I thought. Then, as if someone had quietly placed a blanket fresh from the dryer all around me, I felt instantly warm. I remembered another mother and child . . . another Christmas when everything didn't work out as planned . . . another Christmas when all the inns were full, when the Savior of the world, the Creator, the Son of the Almighty God was born in a stable because there was no room.

I knew that the babe in the manger was my personal Savior. I knew that I was loved and that I was not alone. Christ understood my situation because he had experienced all that I was feeling personally. He would never leave me comfortless.

I will never forget the stomach-flu Christmas. It taught me that life seldom works out the way we plan, and that is the wonder of it all. For only in sickness and pain are we awake to the gift of health and love. The stomach-flu Christmas taught me that God wants me to grow up, to understand that life is supposed to be a series of problems, even on Christmas Eve—for pain opens the door to understanding. My children had a mother who loved them. Perhaps that deep, abiding love was the greatest gift I had to offer. Maybe what I had to give my children wasn't Hollywood . . . but it was real. Other Christmas Eves have come and gone with the more common frantic preparations for that much-awaited morning, but the stomach-flu Christmas stands out because I know now that there is joy even in sorrow, that the daily miracles of life, health, love, and family should not be taken for granted, not even for a moment. In the stillness of that night, I learned that only in darkness does the light and love of the Savior shine brightest.

Perhaps the December of my father-in-law's passing began an even greater personal understanding of the miracle of life—its beginnings and endings.

"I want to go home," Dad said, sitting up straight in his hospital bed. He swung his legs to the side, ready to hop down onto the cold tile floor. "I want to go home."

I wondered if Dad meant his brown brick home in Springville or his heavenly home. I'd never seen anyone die before. I didn't know what to expect. I had been with loved ones shortly before or after their death, but I'd never been in the same room when someone important to me took his last breath—until the Christmas season of 1994.

My father-in-law, Esbern Baadsgaard, had been in and out of the hospital many times over the past few years, initially for quadruple-bypass surgery and later for serious bleeding problems because of liver failure. In 1993, after the open-heart surgery and subsequent discovery of his damaged liver, the surgeon ushered my husband and me from Dad's hospital room out into the hall with the bad news.

"Your father has about a year left," the doctor said. "We would not have performed the heart surgery if we had known what shape his liver was in."

At first it seemed a cruel thing to tell us, but later, after we allowed the news of Dad's impending death to settle in our minds and hearts, we both decided it was a gift—a gift of time and knowledge. We had time to express our love, to listen to Dad's stories and laugh at his corny jokes. We had one short year in which to resolve any unfinished business, to forgive, and to celebrate—a beautiful year to say good-bye.

Esbern was a hardworking farmer, bricklayer, and real-estate agent by trade. He did not take well to sickness and dependency. But those last few years of health problems softened him, and I often heard him express, "My family means everything to me."

So his children—seven daughters and one son—decided to surprise him and Mom with a fiftieth wedding anniversary party during that last Thanksgiving weekend. Invitations were secretly sent out to extended family members and old friends, and we all wrote tributes to Mom and Dad in the form of personal letters of gratitude.

Dad was not a man easily given to tears, but he cried openly at the anniversary party that night as he warmly greeted his old buddies with big bear hugs and watched his house fill to the brim and over with family: grown children and their spouses, fifty-something grandchildren and great-grandchildren, and a large assortment of neighbors, ward members, cousins, nieces, and nephews. Circulation problems had left Dad feeling chronically cold; he said after the party that it was the first time in years he'd felt warm.

About two weeks later, during those hectic pre-Christmas days, we rushed Dad to the Utah Valley Regional Medical Center once again for another bleeding emergency.

All the medical procedures Dad had endured those past months to stop his bleeding had left his esophagus severely damaged. Bacteria filled his lungs. After the doctors drained his lungs, they took the family members into a private room and told us Dad would die that night.

Once again we were given the gift of time so we could call all the children and grandchildren living nearby to come and say good-bye, to hug their grandpa one last time. Dad was alert and able to respond. We even had enough time to call the two daughters who lived out of state and give them time with Dad on the phone.

My father-in-law is a large, strong man, six-foot-four inches and over two hundred pounds, not easily affected by suffering, but later that night as the pain and fear grew too great to bear, he reached for his only son, Ross, and humbly asked him for a priesthood blessing.

"I want to go home," Dad said after the blessing as he sat up in the hospital bed. "I want to go home."

Ross sat next to Dad on the hospital bed, wrapped his broad arm around his father's shoulders, and gently replied, "We're working on it, Dad. We'll get you there as soon as we can."

Dad relaxed in his son's arms as Ross helped him back into bed and pulled the warm blankets up to his chin. Then Ross reached up and stroked his father's moist forehead just as he'd stroked mine in those anxious hours before I gave birth to our nine children. That was when the gentle realization came to me that our entrances and exits from this life are sacred moments of light and wonder, but only after the benediction of pain. I wondered if family had gathered on the other side joyfully anticipating Dad's arrival as we gathered in sadness to see him go. I wondered also if, at the moment of our births, family members on the other side gather in that same mix of joy and sorrow as they watch us leave for our life here on earth. I did not know until that moment that birth and death were so connected, so sacred.

I watched Mom as she sat in a chair next to the hospital bed, cupping Dad's huge hands in her tiny, frail fingers shaking from Parkinson's disease. She kissed his palms.

"I love you," Mom whispered. "I'm going to miss you, Ez."

When the nurse discontinued the blood-pressure medication at the doctor's instruction, Dad drifted into a deep sleep. His breathing grew slower and more labored as the hours ticked away. He struggled to get comfortable. Finally his breathing gradually slowed, then stopped. In the quiet of the predawn hour, Dad was gone. A quiet reverence filled the room, as if time were held suspended for just a moment. As I stood next to Dad's bed and watched him take his last breath, I felt the same gentle peace that surrounds me when I'm standing in the celestial room of the temple.

The nurses asked us all to leave the room while they unhooked Dad from all the medical monitors; then they invited us back in to linger as long as we desired before the people from the mortuary came. The warmth of his body flowed first from his fingers and toes, traveling inward until his body was cold and hard and not like Dad at all. In a breath, what had made him Esbern was gone.

The room suddenly felt crowded, as if we were sharing the small hospital space with Dad's family members on the other side. I felt encircled with love. With reluctance we finally left the room and let him go.

Dad didn't make it home to Springville for Christmas. We spent the holidays without him that year. Somehow, though, even in his absence, we knew Dad got his wish. "I want to go home," he had whispered just hours before his death.

Now we understand that Dad made it home for Christmas after all.

In Conclusion

Home and family, that's what it's all about. Consider how

many families will eventually spring from one mother and

one father in just a few generations. Thousands will be

affected in their opportunities for happiness, their potential

for growth, their personalities and character by the profound

influence of one man and one woman. If we choose to love

before we're loved, to serve before we're served, to remain

open, joyful, vulnerable and compassionate even through

hardship and sadness, we create safe harbors and fertile soil for those who pass through us and come after us.

Our spouses and our children desperately need us to be as happy as we can be. If you ever doubt how important it is to be happy, just ask someone who is married to an unhappy person or someone who grew up with an unhappy mother or father. It's easy to be unhappy; it takes no work, no effort, no courage, no faith. Unhappy people often persist in blaming events or people for their unhappiness, so they never have to face the fact that their happiness is largely under their own control. We determine how happy we want to be.

My elderly neighbor once told me, "If you ain't got a sense of humor, you ain't got no sense at all."

I love her advice. It takes a healthy dose of both grinning and sharing to gratefully navigate through the detours and roadblocks, traffic jams and delays. Family life is heaped with ups and downs, tragedies and triumphs. If we keep both feet on the ground, we'll never have the courage to leave the forces that hold us to the earth, to abandon our self-centered image of the ideal family, our pride, resentment, and ambition, our desire to control or dominate.

If we will let go and delight in the glorious, God-given agency of those we love, we'll find the wings to leave the self-imposed shackles of earth and joyously begin our journey home.